NO SIZE FITS ALL

NO SIZE
FITS ALL

From
Mass Marketing
to Mass
Handselling

BY TOM HAYES AND
MICHAEL S. MALONE

PORTFOLIO

PORTFOLIO

Published by the Penguin Group

Penguin Group (USA) Inc., 375 Hudson Street, New York, New York 10014, U.S.A.

Penguin Group (Canada), 90 Eglinton Avenue East, Suite 700,
Toronto, Ontario, Canada M4P 2Y3 (a division of Pearson Penguin Canada Inc.)

Penguin Books Ltd, 80 Strand, London WC2R 0RL, England

Penguin Ireland, 25 St Stephen's Green, Dublin 2, Ireland (a division of Penguin Books Ltd)

Penguin Books Australia Ltd, 250 Camberwell Road, Camberwell, Victoria 3124,
Australia (a division of Pearson Australia Group Pty Ltd)

Penguin Books India Pvt Ltd, 11 Community Centre, Panchsheel Park, New Delhi – 110 017, India

Penguin Group (NZ), 67 Apollo Drive, Rosedale, North Shore 0632,
New Zealand (a division of Pearson New Zealand Ltd)

Penguin Books (South Africa) (Pty) Ltd, 24 Sturdee Avenue,
Rosebank, Johannesburg 2196, South Africa

Penguin Books Ltd, Registered Offices:
80 Strand, London WC2R 0RL, England

First published in 2009 by Portfolio,
a member of Penguin Group (USA) Inc.

10 9 8 7 6 5 4 3 2 1

LIBRARY OF CONGRESS CATALOGING-IN-PUBLICATION DATA

Hayes, Tom.
No size fits all : from mass marketing to mass handselling / by Tom Hayes and
Michael S. Malone.
p.   cm.
Includes bibliographical references and index.
ISBN 978-1-59184-267-5
1. Telemarketing.   2. Business networks.   3. Consumer behavior.   I. Malone, Michael S.
(Michael Shawn), 1954–   II. Title.
HF5415.1265.H39 2009
658.8'72—dc22   2009013094

Printed in the United States of America
Set in Iowan Old Style
Designed by Jaime Putorti

For
Emerson, who came to us from the stars,
and
Greg, who returned to them
—TH

To
The people of Silicon Valley
who always remind us that it is possible to
reinvent yourself and remain forever competitive
—MSM

CONTENTS

PART THREE

MARKETING 3.0:
The Rise of Consumer Communities

PART FOUR

LOVE MONEY:
The World After Material

NO SIZE FITS ALL

INTRODUCTION

Ex Uno Plures (From One, Many)

In 1971, European social scientist Henry Tajfel set out to discover just what little impetus was needed for individuals to spontaneously attach themselves to newly created ad hoc groups.

The experiment was elegant in its simplicity:

Participants, who were 14- and 15-year-old boys, were brought into the lab and shown slides of paintings by Klee and Kandinsky. They were told their preferences for the paintings would determine which of two groups they would join.

Of course, this was a lie designed to set up the idea of "us" and "them" in their minds. The experimenters wanted two groups of boys with not the faintest idea who was also in their own group or what the grouping meant or what they had to lose or gain.

After this setup, the boys were taken to a cubicle, one at a time. Each was then asked to distribute virtual money to the other members of both groups. The only information they had about who they were giving it to was a code number for each boy and that boy's group membership.

There were a series of rules for the distribution of the money that were designed to tease out who the boys favored:

their own group or the other group. The rules were changed slightly in different trials so that it was possible to test a number of theories.

The result?

From the way the virtual money was distributed, the boys did indeed demonstrate the classic behavioral markers of group membership: they favored their own group over the other. And this pattern developed consistently over many, many trials and has subsequently been replicated in other experiments in which groups were, if you can believe it, even more minimal.

In other words, given a topic in which they had no interest, after an exposure of just thirty seconds, in an environment in which there were no consequences to their choices, the boys still based their decisions upon a perceived membership in a group whose membership list they didn't know. And subsequent tests show that these subjects would exhibit group loyalty based upon even less information than that.

The results of Tajfel's experiments, which have been reproduced many times since, tell us something truly profound about human nature and our deep, organic need to connect with one another. But these results are also a window into the puzzle that has become the modern global economy. It is this irresistible need to connect with one another—at times against all reason—that more than anything will define the next few decades. And it is this deep impulse, atavistically returning at a time when we find ourselves both unmoored from tradition and overwhelmed by choice and opportunity, that is sending history spinning off in an unexpected direction and making a hash of even the most logical prognostications.

● ● ●

We humans are social beings, best suited for small groups of trustworthy compatriots. Today's technology—the Internet in particular—allows us not only to communicate, but to form new types of social constructs based on ancient impulses. Everywhere you look people are connecting, collaborating, and competing in new ways. And yet, we are also using the Internet to destroy what has come before—institutions (e.g., libraries, video shops, bookstores), intermediaries (record companies, movie theaters), and traditions (the morning paper, the evening news).

What we seem to have forgotten as we looked out across the rapidly changing landscape of the digital revolution is that if you disestablish the institutions that have provided security and succor to humanity for centuries, if you provide a nearly infinite number of options for people and empower individuals with unprecedented control over their own lives, the resulting psychological vacuum will drive most people to pull together into new groupings and to establish brand-new institutions that are a better fit for this changing reality. When challenged, humanity doesn't link arms, but huddles into small, trusted groups.

If we keep this impulse in mind, a lot of the unexpected phenomena of the last few years suddenly become a lot clearer.

For example, consider the single most important new business movement of our time: Web 2.0, the so-called social network companies. The best known of these are Facebook, MySpace, YouTube, LinkedIn, Craigslist, and a handful of other giants; but there are tens of thousands more, and they increasingly dominate entire industry sectors, such as video, photography, classified advertising, and professional societies.

With a few exceptions, these are businesses that have never been able to precisely elucidate the service they deliver—at least not to the degree of traditional manufacturers or even service companies. And yet, several are among the fastest growing enterprises in business history. For example, MySpace, which was founded as recently as 2003, currently has more than 270 *million* members. Craigslist, which began as a San Francisco Bay Area online swap meet, has in less than a decade all but captured the classified advertising business of the three-centuries-old newspaper industry.

Yet, ask any of the millions of users of these Web 2.0 companies to describe exactly what business those companies are in— and how they make money from it—and nearly all would be hard-pressed to give an answer . . . even though for many their Facebook profile is their single most important connection to the outside world, and they Twitter on their cell phones twenty times a day.

Clearly something more *elemental* is going on here. These services, and more important our relationship to them, are touching a deep chord in our psyches. As we have just seen in the Tajfel research, that subconscious need is to belong to some group that is larger than ourselves, even if we don't know any of the other members, even if it is based upon the thinnest of commonalities, and even if there is no obvious reward other than membership itself.

So why not just go back to the venerable institutions we have so recently abandoned? Well, if all that these new Web 2.0 enterprises offered was anonymous membership, we probably would. But the genius of the best Web 2.0 companies is that they have learned to use the unique capabilities of the Internet to maximize freedom, individuality, *and* membership in a small coterie of friends and acquaintances—all within the context of being part of a vast social movement. In other words, as a user you get the best of both worlds: the independence promised by the digital revolution, yet the comfort of being among "friends" and part of something greater than yourself.

In the modern world, that is a psychologically unbeatable combination. And it is a harbinger of the future. In the years to come, we citizens of the Internet Age will continue to use our new tools to shatter one traditional institution after another—governmental, commercial, cultural, social, religious—then turn around and self-sort and segregate ourselves by our affinities, obsessions, and passions. Thanks to the power of our new communications technologies, these new groupings may range in size from a handful of people to hundreds of millions. They may disappear in a matter of minutes or endure for decades. And they may briefly coalesce around a momentary notion or may explode into a massive social or political movement.

In other words, the world is most defiantly *not* becoming flatter, but topographically more complex. Moreover, this new landscape will be anything but static, and will exhibit constant transformation—and in its more fevered districts, nothing will be the same from one minute to the next.

What this means is that while, as the prognosticators predicted, we may be defying the old boxes, zip codes, and labels, what we are replacing them with is not a homogeneous future, but something more like an ever-changing, heterogeneous global marketplace composed of uncounted pieces of various compositions and sizes.

This new, Internet-powered process of human grouping and regrouping is not a temporary phenomenon. On the contrary, we believe that:

> *The Internet has fundamentally changed group-forming in our species.*

The presence of more than two billion people (and twice that many to come in the next decade) on the World Wide Web now means that for essentially every person in the developed world, and a sizable minority of everyone else, the rules of social organization have now changed forever. We are no longer bound by proximity, social contract, tradition, or limited information in our selection of the groups we choose to join. And, barring some global catastrophe, this process of increasing social fluidity and spontaneous groupings is only going to continue for generations to come.

So, if we are all feeling a little fragmented these days, it is because this transformation has already begun, and most of us are scrambling to adapt to it. As individuals, even as we watch the traditional institutions we have long depended upon begin to crumble, we also find ourselves being drawn toward—even recruited by—a seemingly endless number of new groups, all of them either begging us to join or luring us with their seeming exclusivity. At the same time, we also feel the tug to join the vast, chaotic, and largely undefined global market being created by the World Wide Web. And as a result, we are being pulled in two directions—toward the intimate and the universal, the small group and the great marketplace—each offering to solve deep emotional, social, and economic needs the other can't.

For the commercial world, the challenge will be many times greater. As businesspeople we find ourselves encountering an unprecedented number of new market niches—that is, those millions of new groups, seemingly popping up out of nowhere and disappearing the same way, all of them featuring entirely new rules of engagement. Not only does the task of identifying these markets seem almost impossible—many will appear and disappear before we have a chance to characterize them—but even the traditional tools we have used for a century or more, from marketing to public relations to advertising, simply won't work in this new world.

This combination poses a potentially deadly challenge to every business (not to mention every social institution and government) on the planet. And no company is either too big or too small to escape it. The big corporations will find their customer bases fragmenting and then refragmenting until they have no way of reaching them; while once-safe little neighborhood manufacturers and retailers will find their once-loyal customers being lured away by vast global networks with a human face.

But what will most shock the business world about this new marketplace is not the growing distraction—even the indifference—of their once-attentive and loyal customers, but the active *resistance* by those former customers to business's entreaties. It will be a shocking moment to many marketers when they realize that millions, even billions, of consumers are joining groups not just to join like-minded others, but to *escape* everyone else—including people trying to sell stuff to them.

This is the second important characteristic of groups, one that we've long recognized in traditional human society but are only now appreciating in the world of Web 2.0. Here in the twenty-first century, to be part of the global economy and a citizen of cyberspace is to be overwhelmed with information. It arrives in torrents, from the television, the computer, the radio; advertising penetrates every corner of our lives, from the clothes we wear to the screens of our phones to the dashboards of our cars; and from the instant we climb out of bed to the moment we return to it, we walk through a vast data field that films us, monitors us, measures us, and follows our movement through the world.

As marketers, we may think we are providing a service to our prospective customers, educating them on the unique value proposition of our product or service. And perhaps that might still have been the case even a decade ago. But now, that television commercial or Web banner or RSS feed, that fifteen-second streaming video ad that a viewer must sit through before he or she enters the next Web page, is, to your potential customers, just one more example of piling onto the mountain of data that already threatens to crush them under its weight. It is an unspeakable delay in their already overbooked day. And most of all, it is one more reason to find a secure place filled with like-minded people—and then bolt the door against folks like you.

The scary truth—at least for companies—about the world of Web 2.0 social media is that it is the most powerful tool yet invented for selective *exclusion*. Once we find our way into online communities and groups, we are far more likely to block out than to let in. And that's the second, unspoken part of their appeal. Whether we recognize it or not, they give us the tools to filter out a large portion of that information noise that is continuously bombarding us; they enable us to construct, as consumers, *zones of indifference* around ourselves to fend off mass marketers, unvetted new sellers, predators, spammers, and the random contact.

If the fundamental human desire to be part of a group drives us to online communities and other virtual congregations, the reason we stay there is because they provide us succor, a sense of belonging, and, perhaps most of all, *sanctuary* from the chaos outside.

A New Reality

But virtual groups do even more than that. They also provide an *alternative reality*. Later in this book we will discuss in depth the full implications of what this means (see chapter 9, "Marketing Is Membership"). But for now, what is important to recognize is that membership in a group almost always means adoption of the personality, the worldview, even the metaphysics of that group.

This shouldn't be surprising. After all, the whole goal of joining a group is to enjoy the status, the reduced stress, and the power of being among like-minded people.

Needless to say, human beings have always done this. From

private clubs to service organizations such as the Boy Scouts to fraternal organizations such as the Elks to membership in institutions such as the Marines with very strong and enduring mythos, our ancestors—and even we ourselves—have joined groups that provided both fellowship and a larger purpose to our lives.

What has changed is the sheer mobility of the potential participants in these groups. Joining the Masons, say, or even the Rotary Club, was typically a long and difficult process, requiring a considerable amount of physical presence for meetings, rituals, inductions, et cetera. Even joining the local bowling team required equipment, regular attendance, and payment of fees.

By comparison, modern Web-based social groups have no such physical requirements—indeed, in many cases members may *never* actually meet one another. By the same token, these groups are much easier to organize, requiring merely a Web address, as opposed to actual facilities, uniforms, and all of the other accoutrements of more traditional groups. The inevitable result of this incredibly low barrier to entry has been an explosion of Web-based groups, from fan clubs to news-posting sites to clouds of mutually admiring blogs. Google any topic you can think of and you will likely find not just one, but scores of groups dedicated to it.

Similarly, because these groups are so easy to create, there is also little impetus to make them enduring. Start a chapter of the Lions Club or a Girl Scout troop and the sheer difficulty of getting the operation up and running guarantees that you will try to keep it going for as long as possible. But when a new Web site is a few bucks, and even a Web 2.0 community costs only a few thousand to create . . . if it fails, fades away, or you simply lose interest, it's easy to just walk away or start something else.

The result is a kind of *social effervescence* in which social groups, big and small, seem to appear by the millions across society, some of them popping almost instantly, others enduring for a surprising length of time. Furthermore, because the cost of entry is low in both time and expense, unlike traditional groups it is possible for the modern "netizen" to be part of not one, but scores of different groups, joining and quitting most of them often on the merest whim.

At first glance, this would seem to suggest a world of limited loyalties, of perpetually migrating members who ally and congregate with others in only the most limited and transient ways. And certainly that is exactly what describes perhaps 80 percent of daily life in cyberspace: we discover some blog or Web community, drop in, toss off a comment or two, agree or argue with other members, share some of our own expertise, ask a question of a fellow fanatic . . . and then move on, perhaps never to visit again.

But that other 20 percent is something entirely different. The fundamental flaw of traditional groups is that they are geographically limited; they are defined by proximity. This is their greatest strength, but also their greatest weakness. You join the local softball team precisely because it *is* local—and even though you don't really like half of the other players on the team, and even though you have to play right field because there already is a first baseman, you still join because it literally is *the only game in town.* As a result, what loyalty and pride you feel for your team is almost always tempered by the fact it is not a perfect fit—and never can be—but a compromise. There is always that knowledge that somewhere out there is the ideal group, team, or club for you.

And where are you most likely to find that special group? Not in your neighborhood, not in the next town, but somewhere out there in the world—on the Web, where you are given powerful search tools to sift among thousands, even millions, of groups to find the ones that are best for you. And if even then you can't find that perfect group, then you can start one of your own, and cast your net out across two billion potential members.

This is the pull that far outpaces the intrinsic flightiness of group participation on the Web. You may hop from group to group by the dozens in the course of a month or a year—but somewhere in that jumble of prejudice, opinion, politics, and desire, there are a handful of sites that draw you ever deeper inside their walls. Some are social networks (such as Facebook), others are platforms for like-minded people to prop up one another's commitment to a cause (the Daily Kos or Free Republic), while still others are devoted to a common interest in a subject, lifestyle, or hobby. Determining just what those sites are for a given person is usually as easy as determining which URLs he or she visits most, or looking at that person's list of bookmarks.

What is important to appreciate is that the attraction of virtual groups can be even *greater* than that of traditional groups. Why? Because, thanks to the way they are formed—by common interests rather than physical proximity—they are far more likely to be monochromatic in their beliefs and attitudes.

In other words, virtual groups are far more likely to exhibit the behavior we normally associate with closed societies and cults.

Thanks to a half century of sociological research, we know a lot about how cults work. For one thing, they tend to be highly insular—that is, they are very difficult to join, at least to become part of the inner circle, but once you are accepted the range of behavior you are allowed to exhibit is often surprisingly wide. By the same token, cults typically succeed because they employ a combination of attractive ("We are a family") and repulsive ("It's Us against the Other") forces that makes them highly suspicious of, even antagonistic to, nonmembers. They tend to block out— often through self-policing by members—more than they let in. Cults also tend to create, over time, their own vision of reality ("reality distortion zones"), which further distinguishes them from others and makes the barrier of trust even higher for outsiders.

Though, by percentage, few virtual groups are true cults (though their numbers are nevertheless large and growing), nearly every virtual group exhibits cultlike behavior to some degree. The crucial difference is that virtual groups are almost never able to enforce perfect allegiance the way physical groups can—to which one can only add "thank goodness." In cyberspace, the barriers to entry and exit are intrinsically so low—literally the click of a mouse button—that membership can never be fully enforced.

Nevertheless, the attraction of being in the virtual company of people who think like you do is a powerful attractant. So too is the phenomenon of *legacy*: the more time you've devoted to designing and populating your MySpace page, or creating a persona in a chat room, or disseminating your Gmail address to everyone you know, the more difficult it becomes, emotionally, to move to a different site.

Thus, even as we flit about from group to group at unprecedented speed, there will still be a handful of groups to which we will return, year after year, drawn by the ties of deep emotion, long-standing personal commitment of time and energy, and self-identification.

Fragmentation and Handselling

Put these three factors together—a supercharging of the natural human need to form groups, a nearly universal desire to escape the overwhelming information overload of modern life, and the hermetic, cultlike nature of successful cyber-groups—then supercharge it to ten times the normal pace of business—and you get a sense of what modern business is up against as it tries to market its products and services in the new "Fragmented Economy."

On one hand, consumers, free to pursue their own self-interest, will indulge in what Stowe Boyd calls "me-first collectivism"— perpetually shopping about for the most interesting new groups to join, even as they abandon tired old ones. Many of these new groups—and the market *microniches* they represent—will be both transitory and low-commitment, for example, "flash mobs," advocacy groups, and brief single-topic aggregations. These market opportunities will appear and disappear, and move so quickly in between that just finding them and reacting quickly enough to reach them will be a gigantic marketing challenge. And even if you do actually catch some of this lightning in a bottle, how do you customize your product or service quickly enough to sell to it before it evaporates?

Yet, because participation in these ephemeral groups will represent most of the time spent online by the world's buying population, you cannot ignore them. You must figure out how to sell to them. And as if that isn't enough, tucked away in this vast bubbling soup of virtual groups are those singular clusters of clever, creative, and attuned people who will prove to be the tastemakers and thought leaders—and possibly your greatest competitive threat—in the future. Identify them early and either ally with them, defeat them now if they look to become future competitors, or co-opt them. Fail to identify them in time, and you may lose everything.

Meanwhile, on the other end of the 80/20 rule are those enduring and powerful groups—loyal product users (Apple, Coke), societies (Kiwanis, Masons), and organizations (AARP, Veterans of Foreign Wars)—whose vast membership rolls, if you can reach them, present the prospect of huge and ongoing revenue streams. But surrounding these groups are tall, thick, and nearly impregnable walls—and even if you do manage to get inside, the citizenry will instantly identify you as an outsider and shun you.

Worse yet, fewer and fewer of the traditional tools of advertising, public relations, or sales and marketing will work with these new groups. In fact, it is even worse than that: use any of these traditional sales techniques on one of these groups and you risk being so stigmatized that you will *never* be trusted by this group, much less accepted as one of its own, again. Trust, it seems, is the new price of admission.

This all may sound crazy, but it isn't. What it is is *irrational.* Irrationality—emotion, unconscious needs, fear, desire—drive the new marketplace. This isn't the old irrationality of advertising appealing to hidden lusts and desires, but, incredibly, something even more primitive: the pull of the family and the clan, the fear of the Other, and the need for coherence in an unpredictable universe.

Selling into this fragmented and wary marketplace requires us to return to a world before mass media; a world of contextual, meaning-based, even intimate *handselling.* Before mass media trained us to think and act alike, people marketed their wares directly to one another in a *social context.* With handselling, intangibles—like reputation—matter as much as products and services. We choose to do business with people we consider honest and trustworthy; we avoid people we consider shills and charlatans, and we revile and shun the criminals and con men. As the next chapters will show, the future of marketing is a return to handselling writ large.

It should be apparent by now that what we are seeing is the establishment of a whole new business world, with very different players and radically different rules. Worse, this new game is already under way—and no one has yet been given the rule book.

Our goal in this book is to figure out those new rules, especially as they relate to marketing and advertising—or more accurately, to whatever new body of techniques and practices is replacing those two professions. Right now, the world may seem totally fragmented on one end, and impossibly large and chaotic on the other; but beneath the apparent chaos there is a structure and coherence. In the following pages, we will explain what that structure is, how to exploit it for business and career success—and how to keep up with a new clock that is spinning at an unprecedented speed.

PART ONE

THE FRAGMENTED ECONOMY

The World After Mass Markets

CHAPTER 1

RISE OF NEW SOCIAL NODES

The More Connected We Get, the More Divided We Become

The instant nature of electric-information movement is decentralizing—rather than enlarging—the family of man into a new state of multitudinous tribal existences.
—MARSHALL MCLUHAN

They have come to be called the First Family.

Discovered in 1975 at Hadar, Ethiopia, the fossilized remains of a group of twelve hominid individuals who died together 3.2 million years ago seem to confirm what scientists had long believed—we humans have been social beings from the very start.

The circumstances of the clan uncovered beneath the unforgiving Afar desert have been repeated in similar discoveries around the world. Small encampments or communities, comprising anywhere from a dozen to a hundred individuals, have been recovered throughout Africa, Asia, and the Americas.

What is believed to be the oldest clan of our direct relatives—*Homo sapiens*—was found beneath the rocky layers of a dried lake bed in Omo Kibish, Ethiopia, by a team that included the renowned archaeologist Richard Leakey. In this case too, the scientists found the nearly 200,000-year-old remains of a *group* of early humans: two dozen individuals who, judging from the tools and artifacts recovered with them, lived, hunted, and worked together.

It is increasingly clear to anthropologists and social scientists alike that human beings have always chosen to band together in community rather than go it alone in a hostile world. Indeed, the dynamics of group formation and the interaction between groups is synonymous with the history of the human adventure.

Fast-forward a few million years from the primordial birthplace of our species and we see that the group-forming impulse remains a vital part of the human experience. Today, we are using the Internet to form new types of groups; let's call them *social nodes*. These groups are linked by thoroughly modern technology to be sure, but they are ancient in their origins and characteristics. In order to understand the evolving global marketplace, we must understand why we form groups, how we act differently in them, and how marketing to the new social nodes is different from anything we have known before.

Spiritus Mundi

An emerging scientific discipline called *evolutionary psychology* is working to uncover insights into human nature—and is already shining new light on what we know about the possibilities of human social organization in the age of the Internet.

Since we can't map the actual circuits of the human brain (yet), scientists have adopted a methodology called "environment of evolutionary adaptedness" (EEA) to understand the external influences that shaped our brains at a critical time in our development as a species. The EEA approach basically looks at what early survival challenges and problems the brains of our forebears were designed to solve in the Pleistocene, or hunter-gatherer period, from about 1.6 million years ago until the introduction of agriculture 10,000 years ago. According to evolutionary psychologists, despite enormous changes in our world, our brains haven't changed much since. In effect, we have inherited from our prehistoric ancestors a psychological makeup that still defines us in the world of spaceflight, computers, and genetic engineering.

As pioneers of evolutionary psychology Leda Cosmides and John Tooby have written:

> Our species lived as hunter-gatherers 1,000 times longer than as anything else. The world that seems so familiar to you and me, a world with roads, schools, grocery stores, factories, farms, and nation-states, has lasted for only an eyeblink of time when compared to our entire evolutionary history. The computer age is only a little older than the typical college student, and the industrial revolution is a mere 200 years old. Agriculture first appeared on earth only 10,000 years ago, and it wasn't until about 5,000 years ago that as many as half of the human population engaged in farming rather than hunting and gathering. Natural selection is a slow process, and there just haven't been enough generations for it to design circuits that are well-adapted to our post-industrial life.
>
> In other words, our modern skulls house a Stone Age mind. These Stone Age priorities produced a brain far better at solving some problems than others. In many cases, our brains are better at solving the kinds of problems our ancestors faced on the African savannahs than they are at solving the more familiar tasks we face in a college classroom or a modern city . . . For example, it is easier for us to deal with small, hunter-gatherer-band sized groups of people than with crowds of thousands. . . .

According to Cosmides and Tooby, concern for basic survival was the prime motivator of early man. Life (to borrow from Hobbes) was nasty, brutish, and short—with plenty of unsavory ways to die. Staving off packs of wild dogs by day and leopards by night, hunting for food, and finding suitable mates were the central challenges of our Pleistocene cousins. In short: safety, sustenance, and sex. Going it alone was not an option; so the impulse to form groups ran deep.

Understanding the problems faced by our hunter-gatherer ancestors can help us to better understand human nature, the group-forming impulse, and the prospects and pathologies of modern social systems. What we can learn from the earliest groups of humans is what drives our impulse to form social bonds in the first place—and how we choose whom to bond with. It is an important question for today's marketers. In fact, it may be the only question that matters.

Flash Hordes

Charles Darwin and his fellow evolutionary scientists of the nineteenth century used a term of Tartar origin, "horde," to refer to the simplest possible form of social group used by our prehistoric brethren. Hordes were short-term, ad hoc groupings organized for a specific purpose, usually hunting and warring. Apparently, those hording impulses linger within us today. Just ask Bill Wasik.

By day a senior editor at *Harper's* magazine, Wasik is the instigator of the "flash mob" phenomenon in New York. A flash mob is an orchestrated gathering of random people, usually in a predetermined location, who perform some brief action or stunt, and then quickly disperse again.

How does it work? The word of an event is spread to mob members via e-mail, text messaging, mobile blogs (such as Twitter), or other social media. Participants are told the time and place to show up and a brief on the stunt to be performed—anything from a shopping gag at a department store to a pillow fight in a public square. When the event ends, participants simply peel away as quickly as they formed, returning to their homes and workplaces. A frivolous, even ironic act, sure, but one that uses modern technology to achieve an ancient end.

Rooted in our old brains is a subtlety worth noting: there is power in ad hoc groups—in hordes.

Linked Protest

We remember it now as the Battle for Seattle.

On November 30, 1999, the streets of the Emerald City became a near war zone of sometimes violent protest over the events of the World Trade Organization's Ministerial Conference being held there. Memorably, the protests—which ran from the farcical (a man dressed in a sea turtle costume became emblematic) to the vicious (car burnings and other destruction of property)—were carried out by seemingly unrelated throngs of antiglobalists. Indeed, many of the participants had competing interests—for example, union workers standing shoulder-to-shoulder with environmentalists who were trying to close down factories.

Despite its lack of unity on many issues, this odd and eclectic horde was rallied because it perceived it had a common threat in the expansion of the WTO's global influence.

As Georgia Institute of Technology sociologist Eugene Thacker later wrote:

As part of the anti-globalization movement, the events in Seattle were noteworthy for a number of reasons.

One reason was that the form that the protests took was not exclusively based on a mass gathering of bodies at a centralized, highly visible location. Instead, so-called "affinity groups"— from pro-democracy supporters to anarchists—organized themselves on a local level, dispersing themselves in and around downtown Seattle, thereby frustrating the containment and control of riot police (and sometimes of the movement itself).

Another, related reason the Seattle events are noteworthy was their use of mobile and wireless technologies. As is well documented, the use of mobile phones, pagers, and other technologies was a significant factor in enabling affinity groups to communicate and coordinate their movements within the city.

While most interpretations of the Seattle protests strictly deny that anti-globalization movements are technologically determined, what is often noted is this link between distributed dissent and mobile/wireless technologies. Case studies, such as the People Power II protests in the Philippines, the ongoing Zapatista resistance, and the international F15 demonstrations, all share this combination of collectivity and connectivity.

While its usefulness as a vehicle for civil disobedience is proven, not every "adhocracy" need be in the service of protest.

Virtual Playdates

The 148 members of the Fort Wayne, Indiana, Moms Meetup are nothing if not passionate about motherhood. This group of mostly thirty-something moms meets regularly throughout the month, providing members with scheduled playdates, a Mom's Night Out, recipe swaps, and book clubs. Playdate meetings are usually held at local parks, the Fort Wayne Zoo, or other kid-friendly locations.

Since it was founded in 2005, this Meetup group has held more than six hundred gatherings. According to its organizers, "This group is a perfect way for Moms to get together and talk about what's going on with the kids, give/take advice, and just be there during a time when we all could use friends who understand exactly what we're going through!" In order to keep the energy and commitment levels high, members are asked to attend at least one event per month and to participate actively on the running online message boards.

The enthusiasm of the Fort Wayne moms' group is typical of the type of casual, occasional groups made possible through Meetup.com. Founded in 2002 with the idea of using the Internet to encourage in-person local meetings, Meetup now has nearly five million members in fifty-five countries, with nearly five thousand groups organized around interests as diverse as dogs, coin collecting, scrapbooking, cooking, Sylvia Plath's poetry, and Christian mysticism. Meeting in cafés, restaurants, libraries, and living rooms, the groups use the communication, calendaring, and collaboration tools available free on the Meetup site to organize easily and efficiently with little administrative burden.

In reviewing the business, *The Boston Globe* observed, "The website Meetup.com might also be called 'when centuries collide,' for it marries the human impulse to gather in convivial groups—which is as old as the quilting bee, the hoedown, and the Grange—to the eye-blink speed and efficiency of technology."

Whether referred to as Meetups, "approximeetings," or Twitter-spawned "TweetUps," these ad hoc orchestrations provide an important update to an age-old impulse. As we will see, loose, low-commitment coalitions like these will be vital elements in the new marketing landscape.

Tribes

At some point, and paleoanthropologists aren't sure precisely when, humans awakened to the value of forming more permanent communities.

Experts surmise that sometime about ten thousand years ago the marauding hordes simply decided to stay together for utilitarian purposes. Still nomadic, the nascent groups would likely have moved together with the seasons or followed the food supplies, still cooperating in joint hunts, but otherwise expecting little of each other. Eventually, these loose confederacies must have realized that there was utility in fashioning more formal communities. In time the groups stopped roaming, settled down, and started forming more enduring and structured communities and farming collectives. Specialization of labor soon followed, as did the formation of hierarchies and layers of leadership.

Of course, higher structure/higher commitment communities brought with them unique complexities and tensions of their own.

We know a lot about early tribal dynamics thanks to the work of American anthropologist Ralph Linton. His defining studies, made during the early twentieth century, of tribal people as diverse as the Hill Tribes of Madagascar and the Cree, Comanche, and Pawnee tribes of the North American plains, observed that a strong group must possess three key attributes: "a feeling of unity deriving from the numerous similarities in culture, frequent friendly contacts and certain community of interest." In other words, being a member of a tribe involved deep feelings of commitment, belonging, and loyalty.

In exploring the relationship between connectivity and collectivity, Eugene Thacker observed, "Connectivity is more a status than a state or a thing. Connectivity is a 'status' in both the technical and political sense of the term. Connectivity can be high or low, it can be wide or narrow, and it can be centralized or decentralized. Connectivity is not synonymous with 'relation,' but presupposes it."

We get a rare millennia-old view of what holds a group together through the experience of the Hmong people.

Believed to have lived in China even before the Chinese, the Hmong have been buffeted by five thousand years of challenge and hardship. Chased for centuries from their ancestral homelands by China's ethnic Han, and punished in modern times by war, disease, and starvation, the Hmong have remarkably—improbably—survived, their traditions, customs, and rituals largely unchanged over time.

The majority of Hmong today live in the remote highlands of southern China, but tribal members have been scattered to the four corners of the world. Yet no matter where they are found—in the remote foothills of Laos or in a major urban enclave like St. Paul, Minnesota—the Hmong have maintained remarkable group cohesion and integrity through the ages.

Why? Clearly the shared culture and qualities that have been passed down from generation to generation have been vital, but in the case of embattled tribes like the Hmong there is an additional factor: the force of their shared hardships and common external enmities has strengthened their sense of identity.

It seems that groups are sometimes best defined—and best hewn—by oppositional forces, what Marshall McLuhan called the surrounding "anti-environment." In short, for members of many groups, it seems that being *different* from others may be just as important as being the same as one another. Throughout human history, we have seen the forces of opposition and periods of hardship actually strengthen communities of people, from the experience of resource-constrained "island" nations like Japan and Sweden, to the centuries-long travails of Jews.

Group Solidarity

By the nineteenth century, the rise of an industrial age economy and society caused great changes in the way communities were formed and maintained. People in Europe and North America began migrating from rural areas to work in factories often larger than the entire towns they left. With the gradual eclipse of simpler, agrarian forms of community, social scientists of the era, such as Émile Durkheim, began studying the nature of social groups to better understand the dynamics of a modernizing culture.

On considering how society groups itself, Durkheim divided our tendency to associate into two kinds of groups: *mechanical* and *organic*.

Mechanical solidarity, as he defined it, refers to those relationships we cannot control—family, long-standing community ties, our so-called lot in life, real or perceived.

Organic solidarity, on the other hand, is group formation based upon "specialization," or preference. Organic groups are the kinds of fellowships we have selected for ourselves of our own free will.

Crudely speaking, mechanical organization is based on what makes us intrinsically the same; organic organization is based on a desire to adapt and change.

Today, using Durkheim's terminology, we live in a world where organic organizational tools are empowering us to restore our largely lost mechanical solidarity. We can now use social media to efficiently create any type of community we want, drawing members from anywhere in the world. Without respect to traditional socioeconomic barriers, people are using online communities such as MySpace, Facebook, Classmates.com, and others to reconnect with old friends and acquaintances (so-called *latent ties*), make new friends, and even recruit an extended network of less convivial "weaker ties."

The rap on the big social communities, however, is that they have become too big to be useful anymore—which has led to a second wave of social networks created to address this perceived weakness.

According to the folks at the online community-builder Affinity Circles, the most important qualities in organic communities are self-determination and exclusivity.

Affinity Circles calls itself "the Web's first private and completely secure online social network." At the heart of its value proposition is the idea that users have complete control over their own communities, dictating who is allowed in and how much access they are accorded. Affinity Circles is among the emerging alternatives to the big, open networks that some critics believe bring with them distraction and overexposure. According to CEO Steve Loughlin, exclusivity is the key: "Affinity Circles are trusted social networks. Our software platform enables users to search and communicate with one another based on a rich profile of who they are and a network of who they know."

Futurist Paul Saffo agrees: "The value of a social network is defined not only by who's on it, but by who's excluded."

Saffo argues that because of their unwieldy size, the big, open social networks are starting to realize diminishing returns, experiencing a perverse inverse of Metcalfe's Law—the value of a *social* network becoming, after a certain size, *less* valuable with each new member.

According to brain scientist and Web entrepreneur Jeffrey M. Stibel, "The real power of a network does not lie in its growth, but in its stability: when the network reaches a point where higher level functioning can develop." And that core concept—stability, sustainability, stasis—well may be the key to high-functioning communities. It is less a matter of size than the right composition; less about mass, more about meaning.

148 People

What remains of the Yanomamo people is now concentrated in central Brazil, wedged between the threaded headwaters of the Amazon and Mucajai rivers.

Literally a Stone Age tribe, the Yanomamo are believed to be the most primitive, culturally intact people still in existence in the world. The Yanomamo live today as they have for eight thousand years. They fish and hunt bush meat with bows and arrows and cane "blow guns," and cultivate bananas, plantains, and cassavas beneath the rich rain forest canopies.

As is their ancient practice, the entire Yanomamo village resides in a single circular *shabono*—or communal hut. Given this propinquity, there is an acute awareness of the ecology, benefits—and limits—of tribal life. To that end the Yanomamo have three most sacred rituals practiced by the village shaman: for birth, death, and the division of the tribe.

Of the three, the most important is the last. Living close to nature, the Yanomamo way of life is best lived in small groups. Thus, for the good of all, when a Yanomamo tribe approaches two hundred people, the tribe divides into two and a new tribe is formed. This practice is not unusual; for most of our history, people have been predisposed to living in small communities.

That leads us to "Dunbar's number."

British anthropologist Robin Dunbar has done some of the most important research yet on the human brain and social networks. From his far-reaching studies of primates and people, Dunbar's theory is that the size of the human neocortex regulates the size of the social network within which our species can maintain a meaningful relationship at any given time.

For humans, Dunbar believes, the maximum group size is 147.8, or about 150. This figure seems to consistently represent the maximum number of people with whom we can have a genuine social relationship. Dunbar further observed in ethnographic literature some common clustering of intimacy within these groups: cliques (5 people), sympathy groups (12 to 15 people), and bands (up to 35 people).

Dunbar's exhaustive research has found that the number 150 pops up time and again in anthropological literature. For example, he studied twenty-one different hunter-gatherer societies around the world and found the average number of people in each village was 148.4.

As Malcolm Gladwell documented in his book *The Tipping Point*, Dunbar also studied the practices of a religious group known as the Hutterites. Like their brethren the Amish and Mennonites, the Hutterites live a simple agricultural existence close to the land. Over hundreds of years, Hutterite leaders have found that the maximum size for a colony should be—you guessed it— 150 people. As with the Yanomamo people, whenever a colony approaches its carrying capacity, that community is automatically divided into two separate colonies.

The same pattern emerges for military organizations. Over the years, through trial and error, military planners have arrived at a working rule for the size of a fighting unit: fewer than two hundred soldiers, in the U.S. Army appropriately called a *company*. Making the group any larger requires complicated hierarchies and rules and regulations. With a group of 150 or so, performance can be managed on the basis of personal loyalties and direct man-to-man contacts.

We find consistency in these small group numbers among users of online social media. As of May 2009, Facebook reported that its members had an average of 120 friends each, while the average Twitter user is followed by 70 people and follows 69.

Are there business implications to Dunbar's number? Bill Gore thought so.

The late Wilbert "Bill" Gore, the chemical scientist who founded the multibillion-dollar Goretex company, not only found a way to turn polytetrafluoroethylene (commonly known as Teflon) into fabrics and coatings used by soldiers and hunters everywhere, but he also devised a unique organizational structure for his company. By insisting that every factory have no more than 150 workers (associates), he created a most unusual—if highly effective—corporate culture. Gore set out six principles underlying his small group structure:

1. Lines of communication are direct from person to person with no intermediaries.
2. There is no fixed or assigned authority.
3. There are no bosses, only sponsors.
4. Natural leadership is defined by followership.
5. Objectives are set by those who have to make them happen.
6. Tasks and functions are organized by commitments.

Guided by Gore's philosophy to "make money and have fun," the company has enjoyed more than fifty straight years of profitability and has grown into a $2 billion enterprise with 8,000 associates in forty-five locations worldwide—an average of 177 employees per location.

Confederation Congregation

At a time when church congregations are shrinking worldwide, the Saddleback Church in Orange County, California, has attracted thousands of faithful parishioners and is continuing to grow. Saddleback is so large that people call it a *megachurch*. In addition to those able to actually attend services each week, the church attracts many more thousands of loyal followers from around the world from its TV broadcasts and Webcasts and from the satellite programs it has established. The faithful are drawn to the sermons and writings of its charismatic pastor, Rick Warren, author of *The Purpose Driven Life*. Warren burst upon the U.S. political scene when he hosted a forum for the presidential candidates and then was invited to give the invocation at Barack Obama's inauguration.

Given the very personal nature of faith and worship, a congregation of several thousand people seems counterintuitive: how does the Saddleback Church succeed at such a grand scale? In reality, it doesn't. Malcolm Gladwell has called Saddleback a "cellular" church. It may look like a large aggregation, but it is actually a confederation of many, many small faith groups.

According to Warren, the benefits of the small group model fulfill a need in the church to keep faith an intimate act shared with a small circle of fellow worshipers. Warren pioneered the now-popular approach in the 1970s, although some say small groups inside churches may date back to the eighteenth century, when Samuel Wesley (Methodist leader John Wesley's brother) formed a constellation of small church groups he called "band societies." Following Saddleback's lead, today many churches encourage formation of small groups of ten to twenty people who meet on a regular basis to pray and talk and create community.

Network of Networks

Ning's offices in Palo Alto are spare, befitting a start-up run by people who know start-ups well. Launched in 2007 by Netscape founder Marc Andreessen and former Goldman Sachs analyst Gina Bianchini, Ning bills itself as a "social network for everything." In reality, it is a free Web platform that enables individuals to create their own social networks around any group, subject, passion, or perversion they desire.

A beneficiary of "viral loop" dynamics, Ning (which means "peace" in Chinese) is expanding rapidly: it grew from a cold start to sixty thousand social networks in its first one hundred days and had achieved a milestone of a quarter million nets in eighteen months—and is on a trajectory to host four million individual social network communities by 2010.

"There are over one million social networks on the Ning Platform with a new social network being created every 30 seconds," CEO Bianchini says. "Two hundred thousand of these social networks are active across tens of thousands of unique interests and passions. They are full-fledged social experiences that are uniquely created and customized for a specific interest or passion."

Driving Ning's growth is its ease of use. Ning provides an array of ready-to-use Web templates that allow users to customize the look and feel of their social networks. It is also simple to add blogs, discussion forums, photo galleries, videos, syndication feeds, event calendars, and other community-spirited features to your personal site.

What kind of communities do we find on Ning? There are a few very large sites—rapper 50 Cent has his own community with more than 100,000 members, while Ellen DeGeneres's community has surpassed 10,000 members. But the vast majority are small, specialized, dedicated sites populated by a small number of diehard fans or one-topic zealots.

"The opportunity to create entirely new social experiences for a specific interest or passion can't be understated," Bianchini observes. "People love to create and join social networks for interests and passions and meet new people around those interests and passions."

Funky examples of Ning communities include the Cult Media Studies community, which is "a global network of students, academics, scholar-fans, and fan-scholars studying cult film, television, and other media," and iPeace, a "network devoted to sharing peace and making a difference." There is the Fixed Gear Republic for bicycling enthusiasts, Global Skateboarding Network for grinders, and Troop Space for members of the U.S. military and their families. Many users have also begun to use Ning to organize their personal networks, replacing a page on MySpace or Facebook with a dedicated community ecosystem of their own.

Ties and Links

The preference for forming small communities should be distinguished from the impulse to expand our casual, low-commitment contacts. Where we may want fewer people in our immediate village, we have good reason to want more people in our extended networks.

Sociologists call these *weaker ties*; they are relationships—distant colleagues, friends of friends, acquaintances that we benefit from in very different ways from our small circle of compatriots. An interest in an open horizon of new connections is also rooted in ancient behavior: the need to keep a lookout for the next food source or watering hole runs deep in the human psyche. We fear scarcity perhaps even more than we crave companionship. And to see this drive in action, we need look no further than the network-builder LinkedIn.

The average LinkedIn member has about forty connections. But here again, the objective is quite different from building a community: now it's the more the merrier.

Community in the Internet Age

By allowing anyone with network access to communicate with anyone else, the Internet is considered a revolutionary way to connect people. But to look closer is to see a paradox of our time: *the more we connect the more divided we become.*

Social networking sites have become the defining platform of the so-called Web 2.0 era and a new means of group formation. Social nets allow people to create their own communities, to construct public or semipublic profiles of themselves, including backgrounds and interests, articulate and interact with a list of other people with whom they share a connection, and earn peer recognition and boost civic standing by contributing to the community.

An important benefit of group membership is social capital, and experts refer to two fundamental types of social capital: *bridging* and *bonding*.

Bridging social capital is derived from the "horizontal" connections we form with people who are different from us but who can give us something we want when called upon: information, credit, technical support, a heads-up on a job opening or an answer to a vexing work problem. These are those weaker ties that form our extended social networks. Bridging social capital is the type we get from online networks such as those we find on LinkedIn, Ecademy, and Meetup. Members tend to share a basic sense of goodwill and reciprocal interest: think Rotary Clubs, where members are encouraged, though not required, to do business with fellow members.

Bonding social capital, on the other hand, comes from tight-knit, homogeneous groups of people with whom we form close associations. Forms of bonding social capital include that which is derived from family, religious groups, fan clubs, or even gang membership. These groups supply emotional and psychological support and may even provide important safety nets in times of crisis. These are high-trust, high-touch communities; members of these groups greatly influence one another's opinions and outlooks on everything from products to buy, to movies to see, even candidates to vote for. These are the most valuable groups for marketers to join but the most difficult to penetrate.

The big established global sites, such as MySpace, QQ, Facebook, Bebo, Hi5, Friendster, and Orkut may get all the attention, but behind them are myriad social utilities that people use to connect, communicate, and collaborate for their own purposes within communities of their own design. Most sites support pre-existing social connections, and merely make efficient "latent ties" that people have already established. Others allow people to form and nurture bridging social capital and to meet new people and expand their personal or professional contacts.

And while the big sites have achieved substantial numbers of members—at more than 200 million members, MySpace would rank as the world's fifth-largest nation by population (China's popular, all-Mandarin-language community QQ is larger still)—the most useful sites are smaller and more specialized. The array of passion-centric sites shows a mind-boggling number and variety of community groups; something, it seems, for every purpose or passion: from Dogster and Catster for pet fans, to CafeMom for mothers, Takkle for high school sports nuts, to the exclusive aSmallWorld.net, designed for high-net-worth individuals.

According to social researcher Torsten Holmer, "a community's size may determine its power to support genuine collaboration and new knowledge creation: all-inclusive membership provides opportunities for individual learning, but true knowledge capital is generated in smaller, less public groups." Yet what big groups lack in depth, they make up for in breadth.

However, the real utility of social media is not only to connect us to the people we want to link to, but also to insulate and protect us from people we'd rather avoid. This is not unreasonable; there is only so much time and attention to go around, so we have to focus our resources. *For marketers, the plain truth is that most social media is a barrier, not a conduit, to connecting with customers.*

Cavemen Online

How does an ancient need to form groups mesh with the new tools of social media, and how do these twin factors change the business landscape?

As a Pew Internet & American Life Project report declared, "the Internet has reached into—and, in some cases, reshaped—just about every important realm of modern life. It has changed the way we inform ourselves, amuse ourselves, care for ourselves, educate ourselves, work, shop, bank, pray and stay in touch."

In the decade and a half since the Internet burst upon the scene, we have learned more than a few things about the intersection of technology and human nature. Some of that insight is paradoxical; some of it is so obvious as to be misunderstood.

What we can say for sure is that the Internet, as a tool, allows us to realize some ancient truths about ourselves and human behavior. We are social animals, and always have been. We are hardwired to form groups. But group-forming is about more than the psychic reward of camaraderie or companionship; it is about utility and survival. We prefer groups that serve our lives in some way; associations that benefit us, enrich us, or support our worldview.

Blogger Ellen DiResta states it well:

Today, groups of people can rally around a cause, idea, hobby or other passion like never before. Even people with very niche interests can gain strength in numbers, giving them a stronger voice and greater power to make things happen. On the surface, it would seem like this is a marketer's dream. Just find these groups, and you have a ready audience to whom you can market your products and services. But it's not working out that easily. These groups have become much more than billboards for the eyeballs they attract each day. They have become thriving, vibrant communities of people who care about each other and do not want to be assaulted by blatant marketing and sales tactics. This has highlighted the importance of truly understanding your consumers. The insights you derive should guide your company to new ways to provide authentic experiences that your consumers will value. You need to become one of them before they will pay attention to you.

Our groups give us identity and a comforting sense of belonging. To that end, we not only define ourselves by the groups we belong to, we define ourselves by the groups we don't belong to. Like our ancient cousins, we gain strength by the presence of opposing external forces and other, even rival, groups. And in more modern times, we have learned to make community, organically, in our own vision, with people who may be around the corner or around the globe.

After the initial exuberance of joining the new rush of social media sites, we've also learned that we can only maintain meaningful relationships with so many people; we've come to prefer smallish communities of less than a few hundred people. It seems that even if we live in a large city, we find a way to live in a manageable neighborhood.

For marketers, politicians, and community leaders, the message is clear: *you must see your customers or constituents in a new social context.* They are using social networks to form small, self-selected communities of interest. Built around common interests and passions, these communities are insular, invitation-only places. Your customers or constituents now advise each other on everything from purchases to political opinions without the need for traditional mass marketing. They are inuring themselves to your advertising and marketing. Trust is the coin of the realm. And they won't trust you—until you earn it.

Like the tribes that defined the ancient world, the next social landscape will be a virtual constellation of millions of small, tightly knit communities—social nodes—built on mutual benefit, tied together by common affinities and shared rituals and communications. And these small communities will find themselves floating in a vast, largely undifferentiated ocean of a global marketplace, filled with billions of people (including members of these groups when they venture out), empowered by the Internet, pursuing uncounted numbers of business opportunities, products, services, and transactions. For all their internal stability, these little groups will in fact be like foam in the sea. It's no wonder that they will want to build strong walls.

In this post-mass, post-broadcast world, marketing will be driven by membership—a peer-to-peer vector of permission. The presumption—sometimes the rule—is that you have been vetted by another member before being invited in, so you are therefore okay to the other members. Community members will not tolerate unsolicited communications from outsiders. That includes spam and advertising and product pitches from unknown entities.

Françoise Sabbah was prescient about the new fragmentation when she wrote two decades ago:

> In sum, the new media determine a segmented, differentiated audience that, although massive in terms of numbers, is no longer a mass audience in terms of simultaneity and uniformity of the message it receives. The new media are no longer mass media in the traditional sense of sending a limited number of messages to a homogeneous mass audience. Because of the multiplicity of messages and sources, the audience becomes more selective. The targeted audience tends to choose its messages, so deepening its segmentation, enhancing the individual relationship between sender and receiver.

Even if marketers are able to penetrate the walls of these gated communities, they will not be welcomed. Members not only will reject your attempts to penetrate their communities, they will resent you for trying. As we will see in upcoming chapters, the key to the new kingdom is to be invited in, to give more than you take, to allow members to spread the word for you, and to stand out as a good citizen. In short, marketing is now *membership*.

CHAPTER 2

COLLECTIVE EFFERVESCENCE

The Wealth of Nodes

Ants aren't smart, ant colonies are.
—BIOLOGIST DEBORAH M. GORDON

In the science fiction novel *Down and Out in the Magic Kingdom*, Cory Doctorow takes us to a post-scarcity future world in which death has been made obsolete by personality recycling, adhocracies have replaced bureaucracies and corporations, and social capital—called Whuffie—is the coin of the realm.

Since material want and human suffering are virtually non-existent, traditional forms of social incentive have disappeared—Whuffie has replaced money altogether as the engine of the economy. The thing is, you get Whuffie from others—it is the measure of your reputation as determined by other people—friends, neighbors, complete strangers: the more you conform to what your social group expects of you, the more Whuffie—social money—you get.

Doctorow's world remains for now a futurist flight of imagination, but as we discussed in the previous chapter, people are forming and maintaining many new types of social groups, making social capital—the esteem and status members receive from one another—more valuable than ever. Moreover, social nodes built on affinity and passion develop a culture all their own, which can make them insular, gated communities. The more valuable social capital becomes inside a close-knit community, the more likely it is that people in the group will strive to earn more of it by conforming to that group's expectations.

Unfortunately, this creates a predictable cycle: the more people conform, the more clouded and distorted a group's collective thinking becomes. In other words, for marketers, social nodes, the defining channels of the new fragmented landscape, are often closed and parochial, deaf and dumb. The very qualities that make a community cohesive can make it self-protective and re-sistant to outside perspectives and information—particularly the overtures of marketers. A community that shares the same views rarely wants to risk that affinity by introducing ideas that could change the compact and chemistry that attracted the members in the first place.

How does the rise of new online groups, or social nodes, change the way companies need to go to market? Instead of focusing on individual consumer behavior and attempting to cat-egorize individuals into artificial groups, marketers must now understand how organic, self-selecting groups of consumers think and act—and then turn that information into an invitation by (targeted) members to join their groups.

"Groupiness"

Before we can understand what makes a group tick, we need to know what makes a group stick.

Sociologists have a five-dollar word for what makes a group cohesive: *entitativity*—meaning the sense that a group has a conscious reason to exist in the first place. A simpler phrase sometimes used is "groupiness." As we noted earlier, utility plays a major part in the sensation of groupiness. People are motivated to form and join groups for rational reasons, and those reasons almost always revolve around self-interest. Group membership must have its advantages, otherwise why bother?

Our ancient brains tell us to form groups for protection or gain, so it starts with a notion of utility. Early groups formed around pure functionality: hunting cooperatives, later farming collectives; safety in numbers; the availability of mates.

More recently, numerous studies have been conducted to better understand why people join and stay with a particular social group, like an online community. Oxford University researchers define a gathering of people as a group "when its members are collectively conscious of their existence as a group; when they believe it satisfies their needs; when they share aims, are interdependent, like to join in group activities, and want to remain with the group."

The findings boil down to five basic rewards of group membership: social, entertainment, informational, status, and transactional. Socially motivated individuals desire to get to know others, meet and make new friends, and grow attachments among like-minded people. Those seeking entertainment from their communities hope to play, find playmates, pass the time away, or relieve boredom. Members looking for information want to learn how to do new things, solve problems, generate new ideas, or make decisions. Those seeking status want to impress others, feel more important, or gain social cachet from the association. Finally, some people are simply looking to do business— buy or sell things, negotiate or bargain.

But there must be something more than unvarnished utility to explain why a group of people stays together. And, when given a choice between several groups of equal benefit, why do people choose one group over another?

According to sociologist Mark Granovetter, the strength of interpersonal ties in social groups could be defined as "a combination of the amount of time, the emotional intensity, the intimacy, and the reciprocal services which characterize the tie."

The fact is, individuals derive part of their personal identity from the groups they belong to (as well as the ones they reject). Group selection raises complicated issues surrounding personal worldview, values, and attitudes.

As sociologist Charles Stangor puts it:

Generally, because we prefer to remain in groups that we feel good about, the outcome of group membership is a positive social identity—our group memberships make us feel good. Social identity might be seen as a tendency on the part of the individual to talk positively about the group to others, a general enjoyment of being part of the group, and a feeling of pride that comes from group membership.

We have determined that the motivation for joining a group starts with utility; members select a social group because they will derive some value from the effort—they might save time or money, increase or gain knowledge, earn rewards, bonuses, discounts, or prizes. But people also want to share common interests with others, to be a part of a community of others who like what they like. Group membership must satisfy an emotional need.

In *Elementary Forms of the Religious Life*, his 1912 study of Australian aborigines, Émile Durkheim coined the phrase "collective effervescence" to describe the emotional state members of a tribe get swept into when they gather together. Collective effervescence, Durkheim observed, is a perceived "energy" that overtakes a crowd of people, causing the individuals to act in a way that is not normal for them.

According to Durkheim, the emotional bonds necessary for collective effervescence hinge upon three things: a common focus, periodic assembling, and collective rituals.

In their landmark 2001 study entitled "Brand Community," Albert M. Muñiz, Jr., and Thomas C. O'Guinn set out to define the common characteristics inherent in a strong consumer community. Echoing Durkheim's work, the study identified three main characteristics of strong brand communities:

1. SHARED CONSCIOUSNESS—the deep sense of connection that members feel toward one another, and the collective sense of difference from others not in the community. It is sometimes referred to as a "shared knowing of belonging."

Research by Tom Postmes and S. Alexander Haslam at the University of Exeter shows that groups can congeal quickly and almost immediately assert influence over the members:

Indeed, induction may partly explain why powerful forms of social influence can be observed in small groups in the lab: Even when these groups have a very brief and cursory history and limited prior experience of interacting together, they very readily develop norms, solidarity and notions of social identity. If this social identity is salient, group members will be influenced to behave in a way that is consistent with the content of this identity and with group norms. A key tenet in all this is that social regulation and social identification are closely bound up with social validation. In other words, we turn to the group to help us deal with and understand the realities we face, we value the group for providing this understanding, and if we value groups they impose their understanding upon us. The relation between identification and validation is a reciprocal one.

2. SHARED RITUALS AND TRADITIONS—Like all communities, online groups must be mindful of the power of rituals. According to word-of-mouth marketing expert Jackie Huba, rituals "are the shared experiences of a group. They create emotional glue. To an outsider, a ritual can be weird, wacky, or just plain stupid. To people inside the organization, they may be metaphors for life, death, or renewal." From the "welcome aboard" e-mail to the currency of group communications to the marking of passages and achievements, rituals are part of what makes a community vital. An enduring group not only does things together, it celebrates a shared history, culture, and consciousness.

3. MORAL RESPONSIBILITY—a sense of duty or obligation to the community as a whole, and to its individual members. It is that sense of moral responsibility that galvanizes collective action.

Importantly, Muñiz and O'Guinn also discovered that successful communities are like exclusive clubs—there are admission criteria.

People feel special when they are welcomed into a discerning group. They get psychic rewards from being acknowledged by the other members who share similar values, visions, and ideas. According to the study, the best groups may have little hierarchy and may even be leaderless, but each has "insiders" who know a little bit more than others and are the keepers of shared traditions and the secret language of the group. Not surprisingly, some brand communities actually form in opposition to another brand—the researchers found Saab owners were vehemently opposed to Volvos, for example. Again, we see the power of oppositional force in bonding like-minded people. Finally, the best groups—they called out as "exemplary" fan groups for Ford Bronco, Macintosh, and Saab—were fiercely loyal and vocal.

Group members often evangelized the brand better than the parent companies did and actively recruited new members. In other words, these consumers didn't simply drink the Kool-Aid—they shared it with their friends.

Frank and Jack

Frank Sinatra was a proud Tennessee Squire.

In fact, he may have been a kid from Hoboken, New Jersey, but legend has it that Old Blue Eyes was even buried in his Tennessee Squire blazer. If you're not familiar with the title, don't worry: while not exactly a secret society, the Tennessee Squires association does pride itself on close-lipped exclusivity. The association was started in 1956 by the Jack Daniel's Distillery as a way to recognize its most loyal customers. Squires receive a membership card and a deed certificate proclaiming them as "owner" of an unrecorded plot of Moore County, Tennessee, land near "The Hollow," the sacred ground at the Lynchburg distillery where the whiskey is produced.

How much land do Squires get? One square inch.

Nonetheless, many prominent business and entertainment professionals are included among the members, even a few heads of state: George Bush, the elder, is a member, as was the late Boris Yeltsin. But members come from many walks of life, and every social station.

There are perquisites to membership in the Squires: special items and offers—bottles, engraved glasses, ashtrays—are made available exclusively to Squires. Each year members are sent a calendar and receive quirky update letters, often with pictures of "their" inch of land. Squires are invited to member-only events at the Lynchburg headquarters, or regionally around the world.

And there are many grassroots offshoots: for example, Squires seem to make good use of the Internet, as you will find online communities on MySpace, LinkedIn, and Facebook, among other sites.

On the face of it, the membership criteria seem simple enough: A Tennessee Squire is (1) a devoted fan of Jack Daniel's, (2) respected in his or her community and field of endeavor, (3) not employed in the liquor industry, and (4) of legal drinking age in the country of residence.

But don't let the seemingly low threshold to membership fool you. New Squires must be nominated by a current member, and nominations are not taken lightly. Even after one is nominated by a Squire in good standing, because of the waiting list it can take eight years or more to be admitted. Obviously, this is not your typical brand loyalty program; it's more Masons than AAdvantage Platinum.

What sets the Squires apart? A common passion (for Jack Daniel's whiskey) makes the membership imperative clear; a perception of exclusivity helps distinguish members from non-members and confers upon the Squires some social cachet; and members seem to relish shared rituals and mythology and enjoy frequent communications from the company and crosstalk among members. Importantly, Squires are proud of the association and greet the fellow Squires they meet as compatriots in a very exclusive group.

The Wealth of Nodes

In their comprehensive 1959 study, *The Bases of Social Power*, John French and Bertram Raven identified six forms of intragroup influence: Reward, Coercive, Legitimate, Referent, Expert, and the closely related Information power. *Reward* power comes from one's ability to give others positive consequences (or remove negative ones); *Coercive* power comes from the ability to punish others who don't abide by group rules; *Legitimate* power comes from an elected or appointed position; *Referent* power comes by association with those who have power; *Expert* power is based on distinctive expertise, abilities, or skill; and *Information* power comes from leveraging hidden knowledge, insight, or relationships needed or wanted by others.

Of these, the most consequential for voluntary, organic social groups are Expert and Information power. What the shaman and high priests were to early tribes, the knowledgeable and well connected are to today's social groups.

In the lexicon of the social node, social capital comes from the number of posts, comments, and links you provide and the number of connections and friends you possess.

Girl Talk

Olive Cookie is "a hangout" for young women interested in all things Bollywood. The site is produced by "a gang of like-minded girls, who love to share gossip about their favorite celebrities and magazines, obsess over the latest fashion and beauty trends, and share anecdotes from their personal lives." The San Francisco–based community has more than five hundred passionate members divided into many smaller subgroups dedicated to the latest news about the biggest names in Indian movies, celebrities like Aishwarya Rai, Shahrukh Khan, Amitabh Bachchan, Priyanka Chopra, Amrita Arora, and Shakeel Ladak (not to mention *Slumdog* megastars Dev Patel, Madhur Mittal, and Freida Pinto).

Olive Cookie features videos, hot pictures, cool sightings, and lots of gossip and chatter. And there is plenty to talk about. As a film industry, Bollywood is twice the size of Hollywood and has a huge global following. Bollywood releases some one thousand movies per year and sells more than fourteen million tickets every day—four *billion* tickets worldwide in a year.

But the members of Olive Cookie don't just want to read and talk about their favorite celebrities, they want to emulate them, be just like them. There is a big focus on fashion; everything from the latest couture to traditional Indian garb like saris or *chudidaars*. The site's devotees share the latest trends and tips and indulge in catty critiques of celebrity fashion misdemeanors.

Since content is all user-produced, the community thrives on the latest video and photo submissions provided by members. The most popular vids and pics rise to the top of the vote charts, awarding those who posted them great cachet—and popularity points. And popularity matters a lot on Olive Cookie. On the homepage is a "badge" displaying the most popular posters of the moment as measured by fellow members. The badge is an ever-changing free market of who-is-hot and who-is-not. By definition, those who rise to this level of group prominence have a very good feel for what appeals to the membership. These are very powerful social positions because, while members might enjoy their daily fix of items on everything from shopping, movies, and music to fashion, cooking, and cricketers, the one thing they don't enjoy is advertising. Olive Cookie carries no ads and doesn't tolerate overtly commercial posts. Interlopers and spammers are ignored or shunned.

This is important for marketers to understand: the community has its own culture, shorthand language, and protocols. When the members of Olive Cookie want to know what to buy next, they don't rely on advertising to shape their opinions; they simply ask each other—taking their cues from the most popular tastemakers of the day.

Every Person a Voice

Despite their diversity of interests and populations, most community sites share certain common features. Sign-up is usually simple: provide your name, address, e-mail address, and one or two other pieces of information and you are up and running, ready to create an online persona. MySpace features an "About Me" section where members can post name, age, location, and other personal details such as sexual orientation, relationship status, zodiac sign, favorite music, movies, and television shows, as well as personal heroes. And members can make their homepages very personal: MySpace encourages users to customize their profiles by uploading images, music, and videos.

Facebook users are provided a "Wall" where visitors can leave brief notes, as well as a "Messages" feature that serves as an in-circle e-mail account. Like MySpace, Facebook allows users to form groups based on mutual interests and affinities. To keep communications frequent, Facebook users can also send "pokes" to friends—little digital nudges meant to let someone know you are thinking about him or her.

In the age of social media, where status is minted by expertise and connections and power comes from participation, scorekeeping is crucial. To that end, a number of significant players have emerged to help people in groups (and generally) calculate and measure status and power. Now familiar names like De.licio.us, Technorati, Digg, and StumbleUpon are the cash registers and stock markets of the new social capital. Ostensibly created to help users sort out the billions of Web pages, news items, and blogs churning about the Internet, these sites also do something else: they provide a measure of what now matters most online—authority and popularity.

De.licio.us defines itself as "a social bookmarking service that allows users to tag, save, manage and share web pages."

Technorati ranks the authority of blogs by the number of inbound links that point to them. Digg allows readers to vote on news items and gives them front-page visibility based on popularity. StumbleUpon allows users to endorse Web content for others to find.

These social media utilities take great advantage of the power of the Internet to give every person a voice and a vote in a highly transparent way. The bottom-up classification systems and shared vocabulary that emerge from social tagging are often referred to as "folksonomy," as opposed to an imposed "taxonomy," such as a subject-indexing structure. As the name implies, under a folksonomy system, members themselves make the rules. For online communities, it is that transparency—the open view of what others are saying and doing—that makes the difference. Social scientists call this effect *conditional cooperation*: people will contribute to a public good if, and to the extent to which, others contribute to it. No one, it seems, wants to be the first to jump in with both feet until they see others wading in too.

Another measure of influence is connectedness. On many social community sites, popularity is measured in "friends." Where members can list one another as connections—making it easier to access one another's communications channels (instant messaging, e-mail, blogs, and message boards)—evidence of one's social mojo comes from the number of friends publicly listed.

But there is more—as is the case with Olive Cookie, members accrue social points by being active participants in the daily upkeep of the community. The most popular members submit new content on a regular basis, comment often, and vote and routinely rate other members' submissions.

Additionally, communities such as Facebook capitalize on the drive for social comparison by offering a host of applications—like a virtual bookshelf—that let you see what books your peers are reading—and "Compare me" functions (*compare your friends and we'll show you where you fit in!*) that allow you to find out where you stand relative to your friends in light of various categories such as cutest, sexiest, and smartest. It's human nature, it seems, to benchmark ourselves against others to see where we fit in. That is the nature of social capital accounts. And the more friends we have, the more appealing we become to others.

Chameleon

Few people have done more to parlay social capital into cold hard cash than Thien Thanh Thi Nguyen, aka Tila Tequila. A modern-day shapeshifter, Nguyen has become a TV star, clothing mogul, rapper, model, and blogger . . . all on the basis of her popularity rank on the social community MySpace.

In September 2003, Nguyen was just another L.A. singer wannabe when she was invited by MySpace cofounder Tom Anderson to join his new social community. To get her profile some early exposure, Nguyen launched a massive e-mail blast campaign inviting some fifty thousand people to befriend her on MySpace. On the strength of her page profiles and photos, Nguyen quickly shot up in the rankings. In short order she became the most popular of MySpace's denizens (second only to Anderson, who is every member's first "friend" by default), with more than 2.1 million friends by 2009. Her largely manufactured popularity created a buzz of its own, which fed upon itself until she rose to a breakout status of sorts.

Her new notoriety won Tequila modeling gigs in magazines like *Maxim* (where she weighed in at number 88 in their Hot 100 List), *Stuff,* and *Penthouse,* followed by a hosting assignment on the Fuse music television network, culminating in 2007 with her own MTV reality show, *A Shot of Love.* Today, Tequila née Nguyen employs a coterie of managers and PR staff, and sells albums, clothing, and calendars from her MySpace page, where she continues to collect some five thousand friends a day.

As *Time* magazine observed of Nguyen, "She is something entirely new, a celebrity created not by a studio or a network but fan by fan, click by click, from the ground up on MySpace. Does she represent the triumph of a new democratic star-making medium or its crass exploitation for maximum personal gain?"

If Crowds Are Smart, Are Nodes Dumb?

It is a canon of the Web 2.0 era that crowds of people are smarter than individuals acting alone. In fact, much of today's social technology is aimed at harnessing the collective brainpower of aggregates of people. Under the rubric of smart mobs, crowdsourcing, or wikinomics, the idea is to efficiently allow groups of people to contribute ideas, opinions, criticism—even money—to a cause, company, or product they care about. Famous examples include the online encyclopedia project Wikipedia, news rating services like the aforementioned Digg and Reddit, forecasting platforms like Predictify, and product design projects like Crowd-Spring. These efforts provide a technical infrastructure that allows contributors to contribute, modify, or rate the value of information to give a view of audience consensus.

On the upside, we know that groups do things that individuals can't do quite as well—like sense emerging trends or threats. And, some argue, groups can—under some conditions—make better decisions than individuals acting alone.

James Surowiecki summed it up well in his book on applied behavioral economics and game theory, *The Wisdom of Crowds*: "Under the right circumstances," he argues, "groups are remarkably intelligent, and are often smarter than the smartest people in them."

The operative clause is *under the right circumstances*. According to Surowiecki's research, useful crowds have three qualities: they are independent, diverse, and decentralized.

"If you can assemble a diverse group of people who possess varying degrees of knowledge and insight, you're better off entrusting it with major decisions rather than leaving it in the hands of one or two people, no matter how smart those people are," Surowiecki explains.

In other words a coffee klatch of regular Joes can actually be smarter than a Mensa book club. Why? Decisions—particularly big ones—require both intuitive and counterintuitive skills, and a homogeneous group of people don't possess enough diversity to prevent experts from driving the bus off the cliff—hence William Buckley's famous line about preferring to be ruled by the first hundred names in the Boston phone book than by the faculty of Harvard. It is different life experiences, opposing views, and even naïveté that help groups to make good decisions; when diverse people come together in a group they create a cognitive ability stronger than the sum of its parts.

But if what if the individuals in a group don't think for themselves?

Groupthink

In 2005, a team led by Emory University psychiatrist and neuroscientist Dr. Gregory Berns conducted a study of group conformity using an MRI to measure brain activity on test subjects.

In the study, Berns and company asked thirty-two volunteer subjects to participate in a test of perception. The volunteers were asked to mentally rotate images of three-dimensional objects to determine if the objects were the same or different.

While in the waiting room, the subjects met four other people who they thought were fellow volunteers, but who in fact were actors assigned to fake their responses. To encourage group cohesiveness, the waiting participants and actors warmed up by playing practice rounds on laptop computers, taking pictures of one another, and generally getting acquainted.

When each participant went into the MRI machine, he or she was told that the others would assess the objects first as a group and then decide if they were the same or different. The actors gave unanimously wrong answers in some instances and unanimously correct answers in others.

Next, the subject participant was shown the answer given by the others and asked to judge the objects.

Would they see the shapes as different or conform to the group's influence? The brain scanner captured a visual of the judgment process.

On average, the subjects went along with the group's wrong answers 41 percent of the time. Now the question was, *why*?

If social conformity was a result of *conscious decision making*, Berns reasoned, they should see changes in areas of the subjects' forebrains that deal with monitoring conflicts, planning, and other higher-order mental activities.

However, if the subjects' social conformity stemmed from *changes in actual perception*, there should be noticeable changes in posterior brain areas dedicated to vision and spatial perception.

In fact, Berns discovered that when people went along with the group on wrong answers, activity increased in the right intraparietal sulcus, an area of the brain devoted to spatial awareness. In other words, *their perceptions actually changed to suit the group*.

There was no activity in brain areas that make conscious decisions, but the people who made independent judgments that went against the group showed activation in the right amygdala and right caudate nucleus—regions associated with emotional salience. Independence of judgment—standing up for one's beliefs—showed up as activity in brain areas involved in emotion, suggesting that there is a cost for going against the group. The bottom line: the unpleasantness of standing alone can make a majority opinion seem more appealing than sticking to one's own beliefs.

According to Berns, the superiority of group decision making can disappear when the group exerts pressure on individuals to fit in.

A December 2007 study of users of the online movie review community MovieLens showed that group members will actually strive for conformance when they know what other people are doing. In the study, researchers simply sent out e-mail newsletters informing members of the median participation levels across the membership. As a result of receiving this behavioral cue, users below the group median increased their monthly movie ratings by more than 530 percent, while those above the median decreased their monthly ratings by 62 percent. In other words, both high- and low-intensity users changed their behavior to settle in at the group's statistical middle.

When social groups are too homogeneous, centralized, imitative, or emotional, their potential to be sources of wisdom is severely compromised. That is a risk of tightly knit social communities where unanimity is more important than objectivity; they tend to produce a conformity culture and a groupthink bias. Such groups find it hard to select the right product or pick the best candidate because they tend not to question the sway of the majority.

In a *National Geographic* article on group behavior, Peter Miller notes, "Crowds tend to be wise only if individual members act responsibly and make their own decisions. A group won't be smart if its members imitate one another, slavishly follow fads, or wait for someone to tell them what to do. When a group is being intelligent, whether it's made up of ants or attorneys, it relies on its members to do their own part."

In his breakthrough 1972 book, *Groupthink*, Irving Janis took a hard look at the behavior of cohesive groups. He found five key characteristics of groups where conformity produced a single mindset:

> The group limits discourse to only a few alternatives;
> The solution initially favored by the most members prevails;
> No consideration is given to minority views;
> Outside opinion is not sought;
> Group confidence in its own opinion results in no contingencies.

People join groups that reflect what they already believe; rarely do we join groups that contradict our worldview or core values. That means that group-forming is a self-fulfilling, reinforcing exercise.

Columbia University professor Duncan Watts asserts that "people almost never make decisions independently—in part because the world abounds with so many choices that we have little hope of ever finding what we want on our own; in part because we are never really sure what we want anyway; and in part because what we often want is not so much to experience the 'best' of everything as it is to experience the same things as other people and thereby also experience the benefits of sharing."

The lessons are clear: cohesive social groups don't always produce the right answer or make a well-conceived decision. A group of friends who only do things with one another already shares the same knowledge and opportunities. Individuals in a cohesive group can be persuaded to make a wrong choice because they want to be liked by the group and because they believe the group is better informed or smarter than they are.

Blogger Kathy Sierra nails it: "It's the sharp edges, gaps, and *differences* in individual knowledge that make the wisdom of crowds work, yet the trendy (and misinterpreted) vision of Web 2.0 is just the opposite—get us all collaborating and communicating and conversing all together as one big happy collaborating, communicating, conversing *thing* until our individual differences become superficial."

But wait a minute, you may ask, what about the so-called disinhibiting effects of the Internet? Don't we behave differently—more freely—behind the veil of the network? Sociopsychologists have been studying for some time the effects of anonymity, invisibility, and asynchronicity on Internet behavior.

In brief, it is true that these effects can make some people feel free to alter their online personas because their identity can be masked or because they can confront people with the luxury of time and distance between them. But these effects don't apply in communities where members have skin in the game, in committed communities where people want to develop relationships and earn social capital. In these social nodes, typical community dynamics remain the rule.

Structurally, an inherent weakness in today's online social communities is the lack of management tools for the true complexity of member relationships. In other words, a group of our friends might not include people who are all friends with one another, or it may include people connected to us for different reasons. For example, you might belong to a social community built around a common passion for liberal politics; but while each person may share that core interest, each may favor different candidates and policies to achieve your common goal. The various combinations and permutations may raise the complexity of discourse—and conflict—to an unmanageable level. If unanimity is a desired outcome, there will be a natural tendency to keep narrowing the focus and "thinning the herd" until a group is formed where all members think exactly alike.

As we examined in the previous chapter, group-forming has ancient origins. Our old brains intuit that we benefit from strength in numbers. But just as old are the natural tensions group membership creates for individuals. Group membership comes at a price: in order to fit in, members to some extent must subjugate their own interests to the group's collective will. And yet, we know that people in a voluntary group tend to want to stay in that group; even the most opinionated or dissatisfied members usually won't rock the boat enough to get tossed out of it. So group membership appears to evoke complex feelings in people but in the end appears to be worth the price of admission.

This is consistent with what philosopher Immanuel Kant termed our "unsocial sociability." According to Kant, social groups arise out of a tension between a desire for self-gain and for solidarity for group advantage. In other words, we like other people, but not *that* much—keeping us constantly hovering between self-sufficiency and a need for others.

Yet once we commit to a group, the impulse to "go along to get along" is very strong.

Acting in conformance to group norms sends a signal to the other group members that *I am like you. I can follow our rules. I am not a threat.* Consistent behavior allows other people to predict what you will do and increases your esteem—social capital—within the group.

And it is precisely what we value most in these online social communities—transparency—that accounts for the impulse to conformity. As illustrated in the Berns study, the fact that we can

see one another's comments and votes sways members to behave one way or another. After all, group members want to please
one another, to win approval, to fit in. Sometimes that results in
members who want to show how smart they are preening for the
community; often it means a regurgitation of group sensibilities.
In that sense, online social communities can provide uneven
product feedback and idiosyncratic market insight.

Pulling Up the Drawbridge

In prehistoric times, group acceptance and membership may have
been the difference between survival and death. Group-forming
was serious business, and our old brains haven't forgotten that
point. For today's consumers, the formation of small, trustworthy
social groups will be the key to coping with a new array of "threats,"
ranging from an overabundance of choice to data whiteout.

But as we've noted, groups are funny things. Group dynamics
create an underlying tension between individual and collective
interests. In order to gain the benefits of group membership, individuals must give up some amount of control to the group's
collective will. The trade-off is paid in benefits gained and in psychic rewards.

And social capital is a powerful force.

When people join a group of their own volition, they invest a
piece of themselves in the bargain; they have a stake in the success
of the enterprise. People in groups perceive themselves to be
more similar to each other than others, therefore they desire to
act cooperatively, feel a stronger need to agree with group opinion, value in-group messages more than external communications, and tend to conform more in both behavior and attitude.

In their breakthrough book, *Wikinomics*, Don Tapscott and
Anthony D. Williams contend that "social networks gravitate

naturally toward norms and conventions that enhance social productivity and connectivity."

The Japanese have a phrase for a society segmented by the media it receives, *bunshu shakai*. In such an order, the more discriminating a group becomes to outside messages, the more insular, protective, and closed it gets. Today's transparent social group formation online makes it relatively easy for marketers to identify and find simpatico self-selected groups of customers. Reaching them is another matter altogether. Even if it is possible to penetrate the walls of these clubby communities, marketers will likely be rejected as outsiders unless they earn an invitation to participate. And again, even with a full-fledged membership, market and product insights gained from cohesive social communities are neither balanced nor objective and must be taken with a grain of salt.

A few points to remember:

▶ People in groups behave differently from people acting alone.
▶ People in groups influence one another.
▶ Diversity of thought makes a group useful, but conformity of thought keeps the group together.
▶ Groups tend to be insular and close-walled.
▶ Cohesive groups are not as smart as ad hoc crowds.

In the next chapter, we look at the new landscape created when groups of groups are networked together.

CHAPTER 3

THE PERMANENT CASCADE

Why Networks Are Inherently Volatile

> Men, it has been well said, think in herds; it will be seen
> that they go mad in herds, while they only recover their
> senses slowly, and one by one!
>
> —CHARLES MACKAY

The morning of Tuesday, September 30, 2008, found Wall Street in free fall. The day before, the market had plummeted a whopping 778 points—the worst one-day decline in U.S. history—and now the market tumbled again in reaction to the news that the U.S. Congress had failed to pass a $700 billion stimulus package.

Absent any positive cues, the trading floor of the New York Stock Exchange became frantic with fear. Not even stalwart and profitable blue chip stocks could stem the tide as the sell-off frenzy fed upon itself. Where rational analysis and dry math usually carried the day, panic swept through the street.

On the same day, halfway around the world, panic of another sort broke out at a Hindu ritual in the historic city of Jodhpur in the Rajasthan state of India. There, 25,000 of the faithful gathered at the Chamunda Devi temple to observe the first day of the Navratri festival. As the throng of pilgrims waited for the temple to open, rumors of a backpack bomb swept through the crowd, slowly at first, accelerating with violence until panic took over and people began stampeding over each other to get away from the temple. In moments, 249 people were crushed to death by the panicked mob.

What connects these two events? Something called an *information cascade*: the tendency for people to make decisions based on observing others around them.

In order to understand how information flows between groups in a network, we need to understand three concepts: information cascades, social proof, and social profit.

Sometimes referred to as the "bandwagon effect," cascades can lead to a self-fulfilling prophecy by seeming to confirm a group's worst fears or shared expectations (true or false), which in turn perpetuates the cycle anew.

The danger with an information cascade is that after a threshold of perceived veracity is crossed (usually when new information stops accumulating), it becomes rational for people to stop paying attention to their own private knowledge and to start looking at and imitating the actions of others. Since everyone is likely to be right about something, and everyone before you has made the same decision, it becomes rational to do what they did. But once an individual stops relying on his or her own information and starts imitating the group, the cascade takes on a pernicious life of its own.

The situation is exacerbated by proximity, real and virtual. People in actual crowds (like the floor of an exchange or a prayer procession) are particularly susceptible to emotional mania. This is yet another, darker example of Durkheim's "collective effervescence." We humans get swept up in one another's zeal. Today, the Internet and the availability of always-on news make our entire world a lot closer and subject to mutual influence. Moreover, those millions of small social nodes being formed have multiple intersections and connection points, making information instability all the more likely.

Behavioral economists have been studying the effects of cascades on markets for some time. It has been used to explain the sometimes irrational swings between exuberance and despair—"bubbles and busts"—that ripple through the markets for no apparent reason. The emergence of "quant," or "black box," program trading is often blamed for the big dips and rises on the global stock exchanges, but software is not the root cause: human nature is.

Information cascades are driven by "social proof." In other words, the sequence of events leading to a full-scale panic attack usually starts with a plausible event or trusted bit of information. In the case of the Jodhpur stampede, deadly bombing attacks by separatists the day before in a nearby state made the possibility of a suicide bomber very real to the crowd. That it turned out to be a cruel hoax did not matter: the plausibility was real in the moment.

"Pandenomics"

The Internet creates the perfect medium for information cascades.

In his book *Jump Point: How Network Culture Is Revolutionizing Business*, Tom argues that the global economy has become highly interconnected by millions of strands, nodes, and information flows, not to mention fiscal interdependencies direct and indirect, hard and soft. We no longer can see the world as a constellation of independent economies, but rather as one big organism, making the transmission of information—fear, falsehood, fantasy—

rage through our body economic the way a flu outbreak surges through a crowded island. In that sense, information flows through the global economy more akin to a SARS or bird flu contagion than to the "magnificent dynamics" of rational market behavior espoused by classic economists like Smith, Malthus, and Mill. Tom called this new pandemic brand of economics "pandenomics" due to its mimicry of biological behavior.

And like a virus, it is the function of networks to spread information. When networks stop sharing information, they die. The DNA of the network structure wants the information flow unimpeded. Many distribution-intensive industries, like the music recording industry, have learned this lesson the hard way. When music became digital information, there was no way to stop it from flowing freely throughout the network, shared by peers with peers. Try as they might to press legal remedies, sue file-sharers, and command settlement fees from students and little old ladies alike, the music industry ultimately realized that this was an unwinnable war.

Similarly, when in 2008 the Associated Press attempted to limit reuse by bloggers of its wire reports, it found out just how hard it can be to rein in such a multitudinous beast.

The network that tethers our global economy is by design as transparent as possible. That is the beauty of the Network; it is also what can make it dangerously volatile. The Internet provides a giant mass of data that must be analyzed to try and make sense of what is happening at any given moment. Having lots of simultaneous and largely unfiltered information is often less informative and more confusing, contributing to the ennui of overload. As Malcolm Gladwell explored well in *Blink*, too much information can impair judgment. Moreover, too much information coming in at once creates doubt. It is as if our old brain responds to this overload with a sense of danger—and when in doubt, we flee. Or, more commonly, we look to others for advice. The frightening part is that the more transparent and interconnected information is, the more we behave like a spooked herd.

The fragmentation of mass media now makes personal networks into very important sources of information. And the exchange of information within a community is a valued characteristic of community membership. According to sociologist Ronald Burt, "seeking information from acquaintances puts information giving and seeking into the social economics of the relationship; it is an exchange of favors, of revealing needs and providing assistance. Whether as a means for bolstering status, strengthening ties, or for showing one's esoteric knowledge, people use information strategically." In effect, information exchange is an important duty of social community citizenship.

As with viruses, the speed of information transmission matters quite a bit: new information is perceived as more valuable by the recipient when it is received first. But speed opens the door to errors, omissions, and the apocryphal. And not all information moves as quickly as others.

Though it is a popular analogy for describing the proliferation of information through a network, the term "virus" should be used carefully. According to researchers at Stanford University, there are "differences between information flows and the spread of viruses. While viruses tend to be indiscriminate, infecting any susceptible individual, information is selective and passed by its host only to individuals the host thinks would [already] be interested in it."

In essence, not all information is the same and therefore the speed of diffusion varies. A deeper look suggests that groups share two basic types of information, one immediate and one more deliberate. A study by Boston University professor Marshall

Van Alstyne and his colleagues suggests that different types of information diffuse at different rates. Their research points to two distinct types of information flows between members of on-line groups: "events" and "discussions." Events or fast-breaking news items move to and from members of a group quickly and often without parsing. By comparison, discussions and analyses are slower in their diffusion. Anything that requires a second look or a second opinion is cast into the slow lane.

As it turns out, this lag time between news and analysis is the perfect environment for a cascade.

Tumbling Down

Information cascades unfold in four parts: (1) a triggering event occurs; (2) a person who is believed to have good data or insight into the event or problem makes a decision; (3) other people, observing the trusted person's decision, opt to avoid original analysis or discovery and copy the earlier decision; (4) the more people who copy the earlier decision, the less likely any new thinking or analysis is conducted. Finally, the cascade loses steam by being reversed or quieted; new information finally refutes the prevailing view, stopping the momentum, or a lack of continuing evidence causes the urgency to peter out and the group moves on to other matters.

Information cascades are accelerated when social proof is provided by a seemingly trusted source. This presents a dilemma when the trusted source is wrong. A vivid cautionary tale of a cascade triggered by misinformation involved the Internet's largest search engine, Google, some of the biggest names in the news industry—Bloomberg and Tribune Co.—and one of the best-known U.S. brands, United Airlines.

• • •

On September 6, 2008, a researcher for a stock analysis company, Income Securities Advisors, punched in a routine Google search for "bankruptcies 2008." Google's search bot delivered back thousands of referenced items—including a top-ranked link to a story from the South Florida *Sun-Sentinel* (owned by the venerated Tribune Co.) about United Airlines filing for bankruptcy. The usually reliable Google bot erroneously gave the item a "September 6, 2008" time stamp. Unbeknownst to the researcher, the story was actually from *2002*, about a well-documented and largely forgotten announcement of a restructuring by the airline six years earlier.

The researcher forwarded a copy of the article from the *Sun-Sentinel* site to Bloomberg News Service at 10:53 a.m. Moments later a headline declaring "UAL Corp.: United Airlines files for Ch. 11 to cut costs" flashed on Bloomberg news screens around the world.

In the space of a few minutes the erroneous news swept through Wall Street: United's stock dropped from about $12 a share to just $3, prompting Nasdaq to halt trading at 11:07. Nearly an hour passed before United could issue a statement debunking the report, and trading resumed at 11:29. United's shares closed at $10.92, down 11 percent—costing the airline hundreds of millions of dollars in value even at the higher closing price.

The Income Securities Advisors researcher hadn't felt the need to conduct independent verification of the Google link because "we are a reading service," company president Richard Lehmann said. "We say, 'This story appeared today in the *Sun-Sentinel*.' I don't think that calls for us to check it out."

Tribune Co. spokesman Gary Weitman said the story did not appear in that day's newspaper, and even though it was listed as "most popular" on the newspaper's Web site, it existed only in the archives; *the file had not been modified or opened since 2002.* "The story contains information that would clearly lead a reader to the conclusion that it was related to events in 2002," the company explained in a statement. "In addition, the comments posted along with the story are dated '2002.'"

Meanwhile, a Bloomberg spokesperson acknowledged that information delivered to the news service from suppliers such as Income Securities Advisors can go out to subscribers without independent verification. The events of the United Airlines stock crash—replicated a few weeks later with a false report about Apple's Steve Jobs suffering a heart attack—unfolded at lightning speed and show how quickly information, misinformation, and confusion can spread on the Internet. Information cascades operate best in fast-moving environments where fresh information—and lots of it—is highly desired but where little time is allowed for fact-checking or verification of sources.

Today, the world's economy is more dependent than ever on integrated information systems that cross-tie the world's financial centers. There are numerous private and public information databases—from subscription services, to government and quasi-governmental reports, to Internet message and discussion boards and blogs. The question is, whom can you trust?

"Pluralistic Ignorance"

But if people are generally rational, how do these crazy cascades manage to get out of control?

The answer is that even the most irrational cascade first passes a sanity check.

Social scientists suggest that we develop beliefs and opinions in three ways: our direct experience, the weight of a compelling principle, and finally, social proof—validation by others. The last of these, social proof, depends upon both the quantity and the quality of other individuals involved.

"The greater the number of people who find any idea correct, the more the idea will be correct," writes Robert Cialdini in *Influence: The Psychology of Persuasion*. "The tendency to see an action as appropriate when others are doing it works quite well normally. As a rule, we will make fewer mistakes by acting in accord with social evidence than by acting contrary to it. Usually, when a lot of people are doing something, it is the right thing to do."

Social proof, according to Cialdini, is most influential under two conditions:

1. Uncertainty—when people are unsure and the situation is ambiguous they are more likely to observe the behavior of others and to accept that behavior as correct.
2. Similarity—people are more inclined to follow the lead of others who are like them.

In 1978 Stanford University professor and sociologist Mark Granovetter proposed that the individuals who make up the chain links of a cascade require a "threshold" of proof before they join the parade. In his view, people have a binary choice to engage in an action or not. This decision depends on perceived costs and benefits to the person in relation to a threshold trigger point: "The number or proportion of others who must make a decision before a given actor does so; this is the point where net benefits begin to exceed net costs for that particular actor." In other words, only after someone sees enough people acting a certain way will he or she feel it is prudent to join the herd.

This phenomenon has been called the "consensual validation of reality": the idea that persons in highly inwardly focused social networks alter their beliefs about the external world through repeated interaction with each other, rather than by direct observation or experience.

In studies he conducted in the 1980s, Ronald Burt found that people typically turn to other people who serve as a reference group in order to come up with a solution that makes sense in a particular context. Burt discovered that people tend to join a crowd precisely because people they trust are in it.

The bad news is that when everyone is feeding from the same information trough, it allows for what dynamic sociologists call "pluralistic ignorance." In a state of pluralistic ignorance, dissenters and contrarians— even though they believe differently— feel self-imposed pressure to go along with the pack in order to fit in. Because they believe that the group is unanimous—and therefore must be correct—the dissenters conform rather than challenge the groupthink.

Everywhere you look, marketers use social proof to convince consumers that they have a hit on their hands—whether it is a nightclub owner who uses a velvet rope line to create a reference crowd, or a church minister who "salts" the donation basket with cash before sending it through the pews, or a Hollywood studio that runs ads showing happy viewers talking about its new movie. When presidential hopeful Barack Obama accepted the Democratic Party nomination before eighty thousand people in Denver's Mile High Stadium, he was using the visual of this enormous reference group to signal his widespread appeal.

One of the most effective examples of building a rapid cascade of customer acceptance using social proof was the launch of the Apple iPhone.

With some three billion handsets in use in the world, the mobile phone business has become a highly competitive one. Even though anticipatory buzz had been building for more than a year, when the Apple iPhone premiered on June 29, 2007, it launched into a tough, crowded marketplace—and at a price point about $100 higher than its next-closest competitor. Besides having a revolutionary interface and state-of-the-art applications, the best thing going for the iPhone was Apple's marketing prowess.

The company that had hijacked the well-established, if unglamorous, MP3 music business with its iconic iPod knew a thing or two about creating consumer cascades. In addition to promoting the technical superiority of the iPhone, Apple set about marketing the phenomenon itself.

Starting on the eve of the premiere, the company chronicled the circus of anticipation it had whipped up. Along with product photos, Apple photographed and promulgated online images of the long lines of happy and exhausted Apple fans camping out overnight to get a chance to purchase the long-awaited iPhone. Apple also showed the armies of reporters and photographers with huge camera lenses trying to get a perfect shot of the action. And then it showed the relief and happiness of the moment of purchase: the near-religious beatitude customers felt with the precious iPhone safely in hand.

Additionally, the company made sure the most popular bloggers, media types, and industry analysts got their hands on the phone first and got to write about and endorse its cool factor in the days surrounding the launch.

The frenzy surrounding the iPhone launch not only fed on itself and created more exposure for the product, but more important it signaled to those consumers waiting on the sidelines that people in the know, the so-called smart money, approved of the product because they went to the trouble of getting it for themselves ("If all these people are so excited, the phone must be good"). Largely as a result of its mastery over the media cascade, Apple sold more than ten million units in its first two years.

The Mighty O

"If Oprah uses it, it must be good."

On the surface, Oprah Winfrey is a one-woman social proof machine. When the talk-show host, magazine publisher, producer, and mistress of all things media puts her stamp of approval on something, a cascade is instantly created. In October 2008, Oprah put her imprimatur on the Kindle e-book reader from Amazon, hailing the product as "life-changing" and her "new favorite device."

Working its way up the still-steep adoption curve trailblazed by products such as the Sony Reader and iRex ILiad, the future of Kindle was in no way assured, even with the mighty Amazon marketing machine behind it. As a result of the endorsement (well timed for the holiday season), the product was mainstreamed to a giant swath of Oprah's devotees—mainly women, who were told that this would help their children be better prepared for school.

The Oprah touch had worked wonders ever since the 1990s on the sale of books: an Oprah Book Club Selection is now worth as much as or more than a spot on the *New York Times* bestseller list—the former often producing the latter. And throughout her career, a nod from Oprah has turned an idea or product into an instant winner (her early endorsement might well have been the spark plug behind Barack Obama's electoral ascension).

Why is the okay signal from Oprah so powerful? Among her circle of admirers, her approval shortcuts the decision-making process for millions of information-overwhelmed people. If you admire Oprah, and you trust her judgment, she provides all the social proof you need to make one less decision in your life.

The new social order will be highly influenced by the few proof-makers who can command that kind of respect. It seems that celebrities, athletes, publicly vetted figures of all sorts can by themselves satisfy the threshold burden needed to ignite a cascade.

What impact did Oprah have on the Kindle e-book reader? Following her endorsement, sales of the device rocketed to more than 250,000 units in the final quarter of the year despite one of the worst holiday seasons in many years.

The Oprah endorsement gave Kindle the boost it needed to benefit from something economists call *increasing returns*. According to W. Brian Arthur, an economist at both Stanford University and the Santa Fe Institute, increasing returns is the tendency for something that gets ahead to get further ahead. "The more people use your product," he says, "the more advantage you have—or, to put it another way, the bigger your installed base, the better off you are."

The clearest examples of the way increasing returns works in the real world today can be found in the computer software business, where establishing a big user base early is the key to long-term success. For two decades, Microsoft won virtually every market share battle it entered, even when its products weren't necessarily superior, because in the 1980s it set a standard for personal computer operating systems that "locked in" consumers for decades to come. Increasing returns rewards popularity with more popularity.

Smart Money

An electrical engineering term, "signal-to-noise ratio," has come to more broadly describe the proportion of useful information to false or irrelevant data we humans must sort through every day. Put another way, we have to sift through a lot of sludge for a few nuggets of gold. The sheer volume of information deluge we must manage has us all increasingly relying on filters, tags, and bots to sort the useful from the useless—and more than ever we rely on advice from people we admire, principally the peers in our social groups.

These strategies may help us cope, but the result is a narrowing of our information alternatives: by our own hands we get less noise *and* fewer signals. But there is a danger to using this sort of coping mechanism. To borrow again from engineering: by tightening the calibration on our information alternatives we risk *path-dependence* and *lock-in*: we become so myopic from our self-imposed blinders that we are unable to make well-reasoned choices. We have no choice but to go along with the pack.

Coping mechanisms are popping up everywhere today. When we use news filters, rely on tagging folksonomies, or look to our social group peers for advice, we are purposely narrowing our worldview and ignoring contradictory evidence. For the convenience of minimizing the noise, we are getting fewer good signals and often limiting important new information. That means we don't get countervailing or alternative insights—we simply look for where the crowds are queued up and get in line.

Even the most determined individualists among us are subject to the conforming power laws of the network. Almost all the news we consume today is a product of a popularity contest—of social capital being expressed as preference. Remember the social meters we discussed in the previous chapter, services such as De.licio.us, Technorati, Digg, and StumbleUpon? Those services provide a herd-view of the world by giving preferential ranking to the most popular items or links. In fact, even when you search for something online, you are being fed the findings of algorithms constantly tweaked to select the most popular items (determined by the most inbound links, traffic, or otherwise verified relevance).

The evolution of the Internet has been pervasively influenced by the existence of search engines. Through their algorithms and delivery formats, we know that popular search engines limit the attention of users to a small set of "celebrity pages." Users are more likely to click through to these top-ranked celebrity pages, which leads to a further improvement or entrenchment of their rankings. Eventually the celebrity pages, even when they are biased or simply wrong, accumulate a constant fraction of all links created and the cycle becomes perpetual.

The Network itself is subject to power laws. Scientists have determined that networks form in a sequential process in which new nodes enter and choose which node to attach themselves to. *Preferential attachment* is said to be present when new nodes prefer to attach themselves to other nodes with the most connections, thus creating a snowball effect. Indeed, real-world data—whether distributions of wealth, size of earthquakes, or number of connections on a computer network—have been shown to follow this power-law distribution rather than the expected bell-shaped curve. This "rich get richer" effect means some nodes end up with many more connections than others—which draws even more interest from others. And so it goes.

Preferential attachment influences the blogosphere every day. As the most popular information is pushed to the top of news lists such as Digg and Reddit, or gets distributed by popular bloggers such as Glenn Reynolds or Matt Drudge or Drew Curtis, it is more widely read and distributed and becomes more popular still. The presence of the power law of preference makes a fertile environment for herd behavior.

As we have seen, in uncertain situations people look around for cues from others in their group. Making the assumption that other people—celebrities, the rich, pundits, well-known bloggers—possess more knowledge about the situation, people will look to them for answers. And, paradoxically, the more times that strategy proves successful, the more likely it is that people will follow when it fails.

Is there anything that can actually stop an information cascade once it has begun?

Studies of information diffusion and cascades have been typically theoretical, or derived from computer simulations. Theoretical models suggest that cascades are fragile: they can be "shattered" by the force of powerful countervailing information. Sociologists call this *disconfirmation*. The problem in real life is that people—particularly when in social groups—use technology or social barriers to weed out such disconfirmations. That is precisely what happens when you employ agents to "scrape" the Web for news on favorite topics, or when you sign up for a news feed or blog syndication, or when you shut down ideas emanating from outside your social circle: you are getting more of the same.

To make matters worse, sometimes the presence of disconfirming facts will simply make a group *more* entrenched in its beliefs. *When Prophecy Fails*, a 1956 study of cult behavior by Leon Festinger, Henry W. Riecken, and Stanley Schachter, showed how members of a doomsday cult only became more cohesive after every "end of days" prophecy by their founder passed without incident. Instead of serving to debunk the leader and demoralize the cult, these events caused the members to redouble their commitment to the group. In the face of compelling evidence the true believers hardened their positions.

Festinger later observed:

A man with a conviction is a hard man to change. Tell him you disagree and he turns away. Show him facts or figures and he questions your sources. Appeal to logic and he fails to see your point. The individual will frequently emerge, not only unshaken, but even more convinced of the truth of his beliefs than ever before. Indeed, he may even show a new fervor about convincing and converting other people to his view.

Once started, information cascades are hard to stop because they are formed in the cloud of uncertainty, pegged to the power of social proof, and insulated by self-reinforcing behavior and bulwarks.

The Cult of Paul

In 2008, you didn't have to look hard or far to find partisan fervor on the Internet. The run-up to the presidential election revealed the power of online campaigning like nothing before it. Not only did the campaign organizations themselves make good use of the Web to introduce their candidates, spell out campaign positions, promote new registrants, and raise money (Barack Obama raised more than $250 million in small online donations), a giant cottage industry of political Web sites sprung up in the froth. Web sites of all political stripes, from the Huffington Post to Pajamas Media, polarized, galvanized, and generally fanned the flames of zealotry among partisans on all sides of every issue and all about the political spectrum.

Arguably, no political cause or candidate generated more online fervor than did the quixotic presidential bid of Texas congressman Ron Paul. Paul, a little-known Republican/Libertarian before the race began, quickly became one of the Internet's most omnipresent—some would argue irritating—subjects. According to data from Technorati, despite rating as a blip on national polls, "Ron Paul" was one of the Web's most searched-for terms of the political season. News about Paul attained a disproportionate presence on Digg and Reddit, and his YouTube channel featuring snippets of speeches had been viewed more than one million times, dwarfing efforts from front-runners like John McCain and Rudy Giuliani. At the campaign's height, nearly nine hundred Meetup .com groups sprouted up around the country dedicated to Paul.

Despite a lack of Republican Party support, endorsements, or money, Paul had something that money can't buy—a passionate following by a small group of antiestablishment, tech-savvy supporters.

In its coverage at the time, *Wired* magazine reported:

To many immersed in the political blogosphere, Paul's passionate supporters seem to be everywhere at once. Editors of political websites are inundated with angry e-mails demanding they devote more coverage to Paul. Blog posts that criticize Paul are often followed by hundreds of livid comments from his fans. Most frustrating to those not on board the Ron Paul bandwagon, he routinely ranks first in online presidential polls on sites ranging from CNN.com to niche political blogs.

Many prominent bloggers complain Paul's supporters have tainted informal, unscientific polls by organizing large-scale get-out-the-vote campaigns through blogs and social networking sites. As a result, the polls are less a measure of which candidate has the most support than whose fans are putting the most time into their voting efforts. Paul supporters say his success is just the results of the wild, wild web operating at its finest, giving voice to a movement that would otherwise find no traction in traditional media.

And Paul fans not only dominated the political blogs and news sites, but supporters also ardently spread the word about their offbeat candidate in numerous community sites, posting daily messages on MySpace, Facebook, and other social networking sites.

As the political calendar unfolded, Paul never did break out of his niche status and ended up a mere asterisk in every state primary contest he competed in. Interestingly, as with the members of the doomsday cult that Festinger and his colleagues studied a half century earlier, Paul's supporters only became louder and more resolved with each primary loss—to the point of even calling for the creation of planned communities dedicated to the Paulian philosophy. It was as if the rightness of their cause—and the veracity of their antiestablishment mission—was strengthened by every defeat.

Critics may complain of its tactics, but the lessons of the Ron Paul campaign are clear: social capital on the Web can be manufactured and information cascades can be manipulated by even a small group of dedicated people.

Systempunkt

August 15, 2003, started as a typical muggy summer day in the Northeast. As the day progressed, the temperatures started to spike. In the concrete-insulated inner cities, midday temperatures flirted with the triple digits. By the afternoon, air-conditioned relief from the sweltering heat and high humidity started to take a toll on the region's power consumption. However, the demand caused no concern for electrical engineers: according to the computer monitors, there was ample "give" in the system. There were no alarms and no reason to ask the public for moderation: the grid could easily ride out this typical "dog day" afternoon. And then something as seemingly insignificant as a little breeze in a Cleveland suburb changed everything.

Investigating engineers would later decide that a generating plant in Eastlake, Ohio, went offline at about 4:10 p.m. Eastern. A strained high-voltage power line (located in a distant rural setting) arced out when it came in contact with overgrown trees. Per the wisdom of the grid, the loss of the one generating plant shifted the demand burden to the next-nearest plants on the system. But as these stations too were maxed out by the summer power crunch, the added burden suddenly thrust down their generators, shifting the burden again to nearby plants. The ensuing chain reaction lasted only twenty minutes, but in that brief span catastrophic power outages rippled through Cleveland, to Akron, and on to Toledo, before tumbling through New York City, Baltimore, Buffalo, Albany, Detroit, and parts of New Jersey. The surge then roared through New York state, New Jersey, Vermont, Connecticut, and most of Ontario, Canada. All told, like tumbling dominoes, 508 generating units fell, 265 power plants shut down, and within minutes fifty million Americans were left to commute home in the dark.

In other words, a cascade.

Military strategist John Robb has called this *systempunkt*: It is the point in a system (a power grid or a market for example), where a swarm of small events will cause a cascade of collapse within the entire system.

According to Robb:

> The term systempunkt *is based on the concept of the* schwerpunkt *(a German term for the point of greatest emphasis or concentration) in mechanized warfare. The* schwerpunkt *is the place in the enemy's battle line you would focus your efforts to get a breakthrough (think the Ardennes in the battle for France during the early days of WW2). The* systempunkt *is similar except with networks. The* systempunkt *is the node in a network that will cause a cascade of failure if removed.*

Put another way, the *systempunkt* is that weakest link, or point of vulnerability at which small pressure can cause maximum systemic failure.

Our evolving social order comprising myriad small social groups connected in an integrated global network is exceedingly vulnerable to *systempunkt* cascades. In a business environment,

Robb argues, "an attack on the *systempunkt* destabilizes the psychology of the market to induce severe inefficiencies and uncertainties." In the future, every marketer, politicians, even terrorists will be looking for that *systempunkt* opportunity. This reality demands a new ordering system, a new systemic view of markets and society.

Cascades in networks are susceptible to manipulation by those who can identify the soft spots. Take the example of manipulations of post rankings on the link aggregator Digg.

Digg describes its function this way:

> *Digg is a place for people to discover and share content from anywhere on the web. From the biggest online destinations to the most obscure blog, Digg surfaces the best stuff as voted on by our users. You won't find editors at Digg—we're here to provide a place where people can collectively determine the value of content and we're changing the way people consume information online.*
>
> *How do we do this? Everything on Digg—from news to videos to images to Podcasts—is submitted by our community (that would be you). Once something is submitted, other people see it and Digg what they like best. If your submission rocks and receives enough Diggs, it is promoted to the front page for the millions of our visitors to see.*

The problem is Digg can be gamed—from inside and out.

Since its launch in 2005, Digg has faced repeated charges that a small cabal of its users often collude to promote stories they like to the top of the rankings and bury stories they don't like. Indeed, a look at the data reveals that the top one hundred Digg users control more than 50 percent of Digg's homepage content, and just twenty users actually control about 20 percent of the homepage content.

More recently, companies have launched that make no bones about manipulating the story rankings. One such outfit, Subvert and Profit, describes itself as a service that allows advertisers to "purchase actions on social networks." In other words, for a fee, they will improve an advertiser's homepage placement on sites like Digg. The company charges customers $1 per vote and pays half of that to the users who place the vote.

The bottom line: tightly knit, deeply networked social groups are subject to manipulated cascades. As we have seen, entire communities can be energized by the actions of just a few vocal members, who can manufacture proof points that galvanize members and sway outcomes. In the case of Digg, the inherent belief in crowd wisdom leads regular readers to believe that the ranking of stories reflects a wider consensus. Those high-ranking stories are then propagated far and wide as true through links and references, creating a tidal wave of misinformation engineered by the deeds of a few.

Quality Still Matters

A century ago, the average person on earth might interact with two hundred to three hundred people in an entire lifetime. Today, 2 billion people are connected via the networked economy, and that number will exceed 3.5 billion by 2011. If you are counting heads, this suggests that enough social proof can exist for just about any belief or opinion, no matter how specious, mean-spirited, or wacky. So quantity may no longer be sufficient proof.

Quality matters very much, and that boils down to the issue of trust. We must narrow down the universe of trusted references or we will be overwhelmed by information and cacophony. That means our social groups become more important to us—not only as a medium for the sharing of new ideas and new products, but also as the providers of social proof that shapes our opinions and decisions. The danger, of course, is that reliance on highly selective and insular social communities of our own design may not provide us with balanced information.

As we saw in the previous chapter, a diversity of opinion can allow a crowd of people to eventually make a good decision. On the other hand, conformity and desire for social capital create a lack of expressed alternatives that make tightly knit social groups less able to make reasoned decisions. Finally, in this chapter we looked at why groups of groups are even more volatile and subject to bandwagons and stampedes. The marketers, politicians, and civic leaders of the future will face a strange and complex landscape marked by new social groupings, new forms of social capital, and wild bouts of social volatility.

PART TWO

CONSPICUOUS POWER

The New Mind of the Consumer

CHAPTER 4

THE ASYMPTOTE CURVE

The Culture of Abundance

> Consumption is a double tragedy: what begins in
> inadequacy will end in deprivation.
> — MARSHALL SAHLINS

*"A venti half-soy half-skim decaf 3-pump vanilla
extra-shot cappuccino with room."*

When we were growing up, a "regular" coffee at the corner diner came in a standard-issue mug and contained generous helpings of cream and sugar. Today, a barista at Starbucks must be ready to prepare some nineteen thousand different combinations and permutations of coffees and teas, hot and cold, in cup sizes ranging from Short to Venti. That a highly customized order like the one above can be served with aplomb at any one of Starbucks' more than sixteen thousand locations worldwide—one seemingly at every corner in any major metropolis—is a testament to the level of personalization brought to the coffee shop ritual in our post-scarcity age.

The idea that you can have exactly what you want, when and where you want it, at the price you want, is an important part of the new social order: we have entered an always-on, always-open age of plenty, of mass customization and ubiquitous idiosyncrasy. And that kind of power is changing our markets, our economies, and most important, our brains.

From Mass Markets to *My* Markets

Throughout most of the twentieth century, the world of manufacturing was characterized by an emphasis on efficient, high-volume production for mass markets. Many of the underlying principles of the factory floor could be traced back two hundred years to Adam Smith's pin factory and his theories on specialization and economies of mass and scale. But to a great degree, by the mid-1900s, processes within the Industrial Age factory and office were substantially shaped by the thinking of Frederick Winslow Taylor, the philosopher prince of "scientific management." Analysis and control were the dominant paradigms captured in Taylor's new discipline of industrial engineering. Scientific management meant that everything in the manufacturing work flow can and should be measured and studied to uncover inherent efficiencies. While his systems revolutionized productivity in the modern factory, Taylor's penchant for order and regulation seeped into the psyche of the age. Indeed, the metaphors, procedures, and standards of excellence drawn from scientific management influenced not only the workplace, but the halls of education and government and the delivery of social services. Society and culture of the Industrial Age reflected to a great extent the gestalt of the factory and Taylor's influence on it.

As author Wade Rowland puts it: "The factory, as the hub of production and employment, simplified the logistics of production and permitted the regimentation of workers according to the dictates of the manufacturing process. It demanded mobility of labor—workers had to locate themselves near their place of employment—which instigated a breakdown of traditional family and social relationships and values. It demanded collective effort, uniformity, order and obedience."

To that same degree, the character of today's information culture also influences wider society.

If the postindustrial era has its Taylor, perhaps it would be Harvard academic Wickham Skinner. In May of 1974, Skinner published a now classic article in the *Harvard Business Review* entitled "The Focused Factory." The concept of the focused factory flew in the face of all that we had come to know and accept about the productive, profitable way to run manufacturing facilities in service of mass market consumers. Instead of a reliance on scale and scope, multiple products and interchangeable parts and modules, Skinner advocated a "leaner" focus on a narrow range of products in smaller, simpler factories focused on one or two "key manufacturing tasks."

In his thesis, Skinner outlined eight competitive priorities for the new focused factory: low cost, high-performance design, consistent quality, fast delivery, on-time delivery, development speed, customization, and volume flexibility.

To Skinner, technology is also an important factor in the focused factory: not just for the physical improvements it affords, but because it causes relationships to change. Improvements in functions ranging from communications to materials maintenance reduce the "friction" in the manufacturing flow, creating new kinds of efficiencies and organizational learning.

In 1977, only a few years after the publication of Skinner's seemingly heretical ideas, the West was introduced to their application by Japanese factories in a philosophy called *kanban*.

Kanban featured techniques we now know as "continuous flow manufacturing," "just-in-time management," and "zero inventories."

The Japanese manufacturing revolution was also based heavily on the writings of another American, W. Edwards Deming, and his focus on quality processes as a competitive weapon. Their use of the quality principles, and a continuous improvement process they called *kaisen*, helped propel Japanese manufacturing to world-class status and drove that nation's historic economic expansion during the 1980s and 1990s. Behind the lean manufacturing and quality processes philosophies is a key ethic: the elimination of waste—waste being anything that adds cost but not value to a product.

Mass customization was a completely discontinuous leap from mass production and required a major paradigm shift in thinking. Today, the adoption of the quality and flexible factory mindset continues to have a revolutionary impact on manufacturing around the world, having been adopted in numerous ways in Asia, Europe, and the United States. Facets of these philosophies have improved the way we run everything from steel plants to auto assembly lines. There is perhaps no better illustration of the application of these principles than the success of Dell Inc. Dell has famously made just-in-time, custom manufacturing its ace card in the brutal battle for market share in the personal computer business. The Dell philosophy (we don't make the computer until you order it) has made it both a price and technology leader in the industry. The company's Round Rock, Texas, manufacturing plant is a model of modern focus and efficiency. Employing some 1,600 workers, the 300,000-square-foot facility is a labyrinth of conveyor belts and assembly stations, its walls festooned with posters reminding employees of the key processes, "Pick, Pack, Press, Place and Press" and "Sort,

Set, Shine, Standardize and Sustain." As testament to its effectiveness, the factory produces a custom-order personal computer every 1.5 seconds, 40 a minute, or 23,500 per shift.

Zazzle bills itself as an "on-demand retail platform" that offers "billions of retail quality, one-of-a-kind products produced within 24 hours." Its mission is to "utilize on demand, made-to-order technologies to completely eliminate the economics of scarcity and empower a truly democratic marketplace where anyone can create and/or sell products with no upfront cost."

The company says it is bringing the principles of Web 2.0 (user-generated content, community, and long-tail economics) to the real world—the world of "atoms" as opposed to just bits and digitized content. Zazzle launched as a company providing customized tchotchkes: mugs, key chains, T-shirts, but evolved to offer "8,407,801,395" different customizable products ranging from sneakers to skateboards. According to its Web site, "every single product we ship to customers is made—literally—one at a time, right after you click 'Purchase Now.'"

The company not only makes the one-off and small-run products for individuals, but its cost efficiencies and flexible manufacturing have also come to the attention of retailing giants like Disney and Lucasfilms with its *Star Wars* merchandise franchise.

But Zazzle has another side to it: a retail platform. After the company makes items for its customers, it then gives those customers the option of opening their own online stores and reselling those unique products. Today, its user community includes thousands of small businesses hawking everything from apparel to jewelry and fine arts posters.

Zazzle—and competitors like Cafepress and Printfection—is part of a revolution in manufacturing and retailing using the

Internet to leverage the flexible factory philosophy. Concepts like customer codesign, open innovation, and crowdsourcing are all manifestations of the mass customization movement.

Many new and novel entrants in the mass customization arena utilize the Web as their prime platform. Web-based companies like Ponoko and Paragon Lake allow consumers to design and produce their own jewelry. MyFactory and Proper Cloth are start-ups that provide custom fashion and apparel. Sole Envie gives consumers the opportunity to design and order custom footwear. JuJups lets consumers make 3-D designs that can be turned into personalized gifts, such as holiday ornaments and picture frames. Tikatok is an award-winning company that lets children create their own books and get them produced in large or small quantities. And eMachineshop is a service that offers users computer-aided design tools to create original metal and plastic machine parts.

But the trend to the highly personal is not limited to Web start-ups.

Nike now lets consumers select the type of fabric and the colors of a sneaker's lining, laces, and midsole. They can also add their own symbol or word to the tongue.

At the Brooks Brothers flagship store in New York, a massive body scanner takes each customer's precise individual measurements, then yields patterns that can be used to make a unique garment. Customers can then pick the fabrics and details for made-to-order suits, shirts, and trousers.

Thanks to new high-tech, low-cost manufacturing processes, Mississippi-based Viking Range Corp., maker of upscale kitchen ranges, builds nine hundred variations of its products to order, allowing consumers to customize everything from burner configurations to finishes.

A century ago, when Henry Ford famously said that Model T

customers "could have the car in any color as long as it was black," he was reflecting the culture and sensibilities of the times. Mass production for mass markets was a social paradigm as much as a manufacturing philosophy. Similarly, when today's companies say you can have it in any color—and offer thousands of choices—that is also a cultural tenet. The audacity of having exactly what you want is a state of mind inconceivable even a generation ago. And it is altering our reality in ways we don't yet fully comprehend. Just as the ideas and attitudes promulgated by Frederick Taylor created the high-conforming mass society of the last century, new ideas like Wickham Skinner's flexible factory model and the mass customization movement are having a profound impact on the way work gets done today—and by extension are reshaping our view of other institutions, relationships, and rituals.

Always On, Always Available

What are some of the social consequences of the Internet as business medium? The Internet gives people more information than ever before—and information is power. And we know that a networked economy presents structural changes that increase the availability of a wider variety of goods and services by a wider variety of producers and providers. This has produced a "flat world," where the barriers to competition have been lowered and more competition means more variety and choices for consumers.

And we know that the Web enables the Long Tail.

Long Tail economics have been a subject of study for sixty years. More recently, the concept was made popular by *Wired* magazine editor Chris Anderson in his book *The Long Tail*. The "tail" in question is basically a popularity curve comprising the vast majority of the world's products. Since data show that the distribution of products follows a fundamental power law— Pareto's 80/20 rule—the "short head" is made up of those 20 percent of products that we'd consider blockbuster hits. Most of the world's goods fall into the tail of least-popular products, from obscure songs and books to lesser-known brands. The large population of potential customers created by the Internet and the Networked Economy combined with very low maintenance and distribution costs means that every product can remain available forever. Thus is created a world of non-zero-sum, abundant thinking.

In his book, Anderson describes three conditions critical to Long Tail profits: drastically reduced costs of creation (made possible by the Internet itself), increased ease of distribution, and search engines employing "filters" and user recommendations that make all of what is available accessible and easy to acquire by potential consumers. The presence of these forces today creates what Anderson calls "a culture unfiltered by economic scarcity."

According to James Heskett, professor emeritus at Harvard Business School, "In the Long Tail, money is made by such things as avoiding inventory, producing to order, letting customers do the work, pricing creatively and flexibly to various customers, utilizing a variety of distribution methods, sharing information, trusting the market to do your job, and understanding the 'power of free' combined with money-making services or products."

The leading beneficiaries of the Long Tail are so-called information goods, digital products that experience little or no marginal cost, have few limitations on their use, and are "nonrivalrous"—consumption by one person does not impede consumption by another. But any type of highly specialized or low demand products can benefit from a long-tail marketing infrastructure.

Amazon.com has made a science of the Long Tail by offering millions of obscure books (and a wide range of other products) that would be impossible to find in brick and mortar stores, or not for long if they did stock them. The same can be said of online movie rental company Netflix. Besides the convenience factor of by-mail DVDs, the company can offer a wider variety of hard-to-find and special-interest films than would be practical at any neighborhood location.

Long Tail, Big Feet

The Long Tail can make life a lot easier for some people.

Take the case of Swede Fredrik Hammarqvist: he's got big feet. His size 14 pedals make it challenging for him to find fashionable footwear in mainstream retail outlets. Figuring a lot of other people—in and out of Sweden—face the same problem, he started his own online shoe company, Grand Shoes, selling high-quality, fashion-forward shoes starting at size 13 and going up from there. The low relative demand (not to mention space-consuming size) of outsized shoes makes it impractical for most shoe stores and department stores to carry much in the way of variety in the upper size ranges. Thanks to the elimination of inventory concerns for Hammarqvist, he can offer hundreds of styles and colors and ship them anywhere in the world. One of his first marketing acts was to contact all four hundred professional and amateur basketball teams in Sweden. Since then the word has spread to sports teams and other consumers around the world.

How "Free" Became a Price

Before the Internet, every school kid knew that you got what you paid for and that there is no such thing as a free lunch. Today, the Internet's principal model is free—free information, free exchange, free e-mail, services, and tools. Moreover, consumers bristle at the idea of paying for anything online; a majority of people polled say they'd refuse to plunk down even a dime for services and content they believe they are entitled to get for free.

How did we get such a notion stuck in our heads? First, the Internet was built as a public benefit using public funds by academics and researchers (many of whom, like Douglas Engelbart and Ted Nelson, possessed an antiestablishment bent) as a means of freely communicating among colleagues. Then, as the nascent Web went mainstream, its pioneers offered free services and utilities—paid for sometimes by advertising—to lure early adopters. Come, try it out, we'll figure out how to make money from you later. The problem is, the free ethos stuck.

It became a question that confounded many during the dot-com boom: if access to all Web sites is essentially free, then how do you make money? Many companies could not figure it out and they went belly-up. But many plucky companies did figure out how to monetize free. Most made money by exchanging content or services for eyeballs—advertising revenue. Some of the biggest names on the Internet have made advertising-subsidized free work for them—Google, Flickr, Hotmail.

Some outfits have begun to make money by offering free stuff as a loss leader. This is called the *"freemium"* model: give away basic services for free but up-sell and charge a premium for advanced or special features. Venture capitalist and blogger Fred Wilson describes the model this way: "Give your service away for

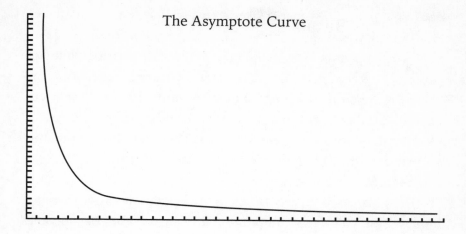

The Asymptote Curve

free, possibly ad supported but maybe not, acquire a lot of customers very efficiently through word of mouth, referral networks, organic search marketing, etc., then offer premium priced value added services or an enhanced version of your service to your customer base."

There is an internal logic called the Asymptote Curve that some use to describe why free works.

Simply put, an asymptote is a linear boundary that a curve gets very close to, but never reaches. The economic (as opposed to the original geometric) theory of asymptotes goes like this: since just about everything will eventually become a commodity, and its price will arc perilously close to the zero price line (the asymptote), rather than fight the inevitable, use it to your advantage.

Former *Wired* magazine editor Kevin Kelly has written: "Anything that can be replicated will have a price that will tend toward zero, or free. While the cost may never reach free, it approaches the free in a curve called an asymptote. Ubiquity drives increasing returns in the network economy. The question becomes: What is the most cost-effective way to achieve ubiquity? And the answer is: give things away. Make them free."

In other words, use abundance to create scarcity. In a bit of pixel logic, free works on the Internet something like this: by inundating consumers with so much free stuff that they can't pay attention to but a fraction of it, the things they do pay attention to become very valuable to advertisers. Then the idea is to charge advertisers royally for access to this scarcest of all natural resources, consumer attention.

The breadth of the Internet audience makes it easier to make money by giving away the commodity in order to sell people something else. An example can be seen in the pricing strategy at Europe-based airline Ryan Air. In November 2008, the airline announced it would be offering $15 flights to and from the United States and Europe. With the unpredictable cost of fuel and other expenses, how can they do that? What's the catch? While the ticket to a seat cost next to nothing, passengers have to pay for everything else related to the flight—baggage handling, all food and beverages, and entertainment. And since the passengers comprise a captive audience for several hours, Ryan uses the dead time to sell products and run advertising. The travel incidentals, product sales, and advertising revenues more than make up for the lost ticket revenue.

It is typical among complementary goods that the demand for one item increases when the price of its counterpart decreases. So the free paradigm is clear: give the experience away but charge royally for the snacks.

The Culture of Abundance

In *The End of Education*, Neil Postman observed that "Embedded in every technology there is a powerful idea, sometimes two or three powerful ideas. Like language itself, a technology predisposes us to favor and value certain perspectives and accomplishments and to subordinate others. Every technology has a philosophy, which is given expression in how the technology makes people use their minds, in what it makes us do with our bodies, in how it codifies the world, in which of our senses it amplifies, in which of our emotional and intellectual tendencies it disregards."

What are the powerful ideas behind the Internet? The way of the Internet provides an entirely new metaphor and social structure that emphasizes immediacy, brevity, and nonlinearity, deemphasizes distance and matter, and in the interest of free play and open conversations, seemingly has a high tolerance for ambiguous, equivocal, and downright dubious information—exerting profound consequences on the way individuals think and act and the way society structures interactions.

One of the Internet's big ideas is abundance, but what is the psychological and social fallout of believing that somewhere in the world someone will fulfill your every desire? What does it mean to go online expecting anything we want whenever we want it? How can we prize something that is given away freely? In other words, what is this new abundant thinking doing to our heads?

Yes, all tools are catalysts: we make our tools and then they remake us. The Internet that affords us new powers to communicate, collaborate, and form communities is unavoidably remaking our society. As the unique culture of the Industrial Age did a century ago, the topology, properties, and grand logic of the Internet are reinventing the way we think, learn, live, work, and play. Some of the changes are very positive; others less so.

On the positive side, the Internet has given us unprecedented control: with a few clicks and keystrokes we can do and buy and make virtually anything we can imagine. Moreover, information is no longer held by the few to the disadvantage of the many; today it is nearly impossible for the old elites to hoard information—not even the traditional media. We cannot help but feel enormous personal power from this newfound faculty.

But power comes at a price. There are trade-offs, and empowerment is not a zero-sum proposition. On a psychic level, having everything we want raises complex feelings. Such power has an odd impact on us humans; through thousands of years of training our brains were designed to cope with scarcity and uncertainty. Omnipotence and abundance can be a troubling concept to fully grasp. We may not be fully prepared for the moral dilemmas we will face, or to reconcile the corruptions of power.

But, ready or not, just as scientific management shaped our society during the Industrial Age, Internet empowerment promises to mold the next social order.

So what is the emerging culture of the Internet order? First, the positive dimensions. The logic of the Internet has given us:

- ▶ A desire to connect with people and create community.
- ▶ A presumption of abundance, rather than a fear of rationed scarcity.
- ▶ A preference for openness and transparency, rather than hoarding assets and information.
- ▶ A willingness to learn from, and interact with, the world at large.
- ▶ A bias to experimentation and a forgiveness of failure.

But these imperatives have their consequences:

- ▶ Online social communities, as we have seen, can be insular and parochial.
- ▶ Abundance thinking can lead to cognitive dissonance and false expectations of immediate gratification.
- ▶ The rise of citizen media can come at the expense of truth and reason.
- ▶ A premise that information shall be *free* devalues the work of artists and original thinkers.
- ▶ Personal power can lead to delusions of grandeur.

At the turn of the nineteenth century, social scientist Thorstein Veblen coined the term *conspicuous consumption* to define the attainment of status through consumerism. Today the paradigm has shifted to *conspicuous power*—to be savvy and sophisticated consumers today means wielding the power to have exactly what we want, when, where, and on the precise terms we define.

There is a paradox to this abundance: we can be freed by our new power but not satisfied by it. As author Daniel Pink has written: "Liberated by this prosperity but not fulfilled by it, more people are searching for meaning. From the mainstream embrace of such once-exotic practices as yoga and meditation to the rise of spirituality in the workplace to the influence of evangelism in pop culture and politics, the quest for meaning and purpose has become an integral part of everyday life. And that will only intensify as the first children of abundance, the baby boomers, realize that they have more of their lives behind them than ahead. In both business and personal life, now that our left-brain needs have largely been sated, our right-brain yearnings will demand to be fed."

As we will see in the conclusion to this book, abundant thinking can lead to a spiritual void when you realize that you actually can acquire anything you want but in the end it won't make you truly happy. Like that line approaching achingly close to the asymptote without reaching it, we may get everything we want and find we did not get what we need. That possibility may lead to a deeper search for meaning as the new order emerges.

CHAPTER 5

MASHED UP MINDSET

Why Categories Can No Longer Hold Things

We are as gods and might as well get used to it.
—STEWART BRAND, *Whole Earth Catalog*

When, in the 1970s, Nathan Schwartz renamed his Abington Shoe Company "Timberland" in recognition of his highly popular line of waterproof field boots of the same name, he had no idea that his footwear—and the brand—would two decades later become an intrinsic part of American urban life. But the iconic blond leather boot (and its many derivatives) is today an essential accoutrement of hip-hop attire worn by men and women in inner cities everywhere. How did a New England hunting boot become a fixture of urban lifestyle? Comfort, utility, durability? No. In a word: irony.

While the waterproof finish may be useful in the harsh city winters and the steel toes a deterrent to street fights, the truth is Timberland boots are popular in hip-hop nation precisely because they don't belong there. Meanwhile, in any suburban mall you will run across middle-class white kids in baggy pants, Phat Farm T-shirts, and sideways baseball caps. It seems that consumers love to challenge expectations.

A more controversial juxtaposition of fashion as irony has

been the adoption by global hipsters of the kaffiyeh scarf. The kaffiyeh has its roots in the Palestinian independence movement of the 1930s, and was revived in the 1970s by Palestine Libera- tion Organization leader Yasir Arafat. Today, the red or black checkered scarf frequently identifies the political parties in the region, such as Fatah or Hamas. The kaffiyeh's appropriation by twenty-something urbanites may have begun as an attempt to show sympathy for Palestinians, but it quickly became just another symbol of "peasant" chic—along with "wife beater" T-shirts, Pabst Blue Ribbon beer, and Parliament cigarettes— by wealthy white kids looking more to make a statement about their power to consume and wear whatever they want than to exhibit any true political conviction.

Like the paradigm shift from mass production to flexible manufacturing twenty years ago, the empowering tools of the Internet Age have spawned an altogether new worldview: *the mashup mindset*. This new worldview gives the consumer the power and the permission to blend and remix, rework and blur, cut, paste, and collage at will.

To see the implications of this consumer empowerment on a market, you need look no farther than the recorded music industry.

The fate of the music business has always been inexorably linked to changes in technology—the transition fifty years ago from 78 rpm vinyl to 33 rpm and 45 rpm was nearly as wrench- ing in the marketplace as the transition from CDs to digital is today. In fact, the blood feud between the two titans of the day, Columbia and RCA, makes the brass-knuckle tactics by the Recording Industry Association of America against illegal down- loaders seem downright genteel by comparison.

In this current transition, once music went from analog to digital, the consumers took over. First were the cutting-edge rap and hip-hop performers who continued to push both artistic and legal boundaries with their sampling and remixes. Then, while the RIAA failed to stem the tide of peer-to-peer file sharing over the Internet, new software and hardware gave the everyday consumer the power to operate a recording studio from his or her desktop computer. Affordable music editing technology such as Pro Tools, Acid, and Cubase allows anyone to deconstruct music files and recombine two or more songs to create something entirely new. The empowering of amateurs to buy, share, manipulate, and reconstruct an original composition from existing work complicated the legal picture, but more important, it fundamentally changed the producer-consumer relationship. Now the lines were blurred, and as we soon discovered, any digital media could be thrown into the high-speed blender that is Internet culture.

Read/Write

Stanford law professor Lawrence Lessig, a longtime advocate for reforms in our archaic copyright and patent regulations, uses two software terms, "Read Only" and "Read/Write," to distinguish the old logic of analog media from the new age of digital media. These terms define the rights of readers to alter code they have acquired. Read Only media is locked; it is to be consumed unchanged. With Read/Write privileges, the user is permitted to both read and modify media.

For hundreds of years, media was Read Only—consumed passively without participation. According to Lessig, those limitations defined our experience and culture: "We listen to music. We watch a movie. We read a book. With each we're not expected to do much more than simply consume. We might re-enact a dance from a movie. Or we might quote a passage from the book in a letter to a friend. But in the main, this kind of culture is experienced through the act of consumption. There's a beginning, a middle, and an end to that consumption. Once we've finished it, we put the work away."

With the arrival of digital media all of that has changed. Where copies of analog media might be inferior, copying digital files required no compromise in quality. Where duplicating vinyl records may have been prohibitively difficult, copying an MP3 file is easy and effortless. While writing marginal notes in a book might have personalized the reading experience, annotating digitally allows for a far richer relationship with the text without obscuring it.

Television provides an excellent example of how our relationship with media has changed. While the volume of TV content consumed by viewers has grown over the past decade, an increasing proportion of TV is being accessed and viewed in nontraditional ways. Video-on-demand (VOD), digital video recorders (DVRs), the Web, and 3G mobile phones are new ways for consumers to watch content. Analyst firm eMarketer estimates that by 2012 nearly 25 percent of all TV content watched will be time-shifted, either on-demand, on the Web, or on a mobile device. Today's viewers are not captives of schedules or formats or even advertisers.

This power has enormous consequences. First, it changes the old business models, upsetting the status quo of the passive consumer enjoying twenty-two minutes of sitcom content in exchange for watching eight minutes of commercials. Traditional broadcasters and advertisers are under enormous pressure to write a new contract with the empowered viewer.

This new power also changes—irrevocably—consumer expectations. Lessig again: "The expectation of access on demand builds slowly, and it builds differently across generations. But at a certain point, perfect access (meaning the ability to get whatever you want, whenever you want it) will seem obvious. And when it seems obvious, anything that resists that expectation will seem ridiculous."

All Mashed Up

We clearly live in a Read/Write world. Sometimes termed the "programmable" or the "recombinant" Web, the Web 2.0 era has introduced a philosophy of mashing—sharing ideas and code, building on what others have made and combining existing things to produce new ones. Wikipedia defines mashups as a "combination of different types of content or data, usually from different sources, to create something new." Today, it has become simple to manipulate code and information—application programming interfaces or APIs—to recreate new and useful Web features.

Search engine Google has been a pioneer in the mashup movement, allowing users to freely mix and match its maps with news, photos, shopping, social and romantic networking, sports, travel, video, and weather to create a very unique and local experience. Map-based mashups are particularly useful, visually displaying everything from crime statistics to strip clubs to the best cycling routes.

Some of the most popular applications are those by real estate–related companies. An example is MyApartmentMaps. com. It updates throughout the day with publicly available data on apartment listings, each location identified by pushpins on Google Maps. The service also finds nearby grocery stores, laundries, restaurants, and other neighborhood amenities.

Another mashup, Dopplr, lets you share your travel plans with friends and colleagues. Mashing online calendars and social networks, the service then alerts you when people in your extended network are traveling to the same destination at the same time.

But mashups aren't just for consumer applications; there is a growing movement inside the enterprise as well. Mashup platforms that make it easier for consumers to create unique applications—such as Yahoo! Pipes, Dapper, or Microsoft Popfly—are beginning to find a home inside companies.

Sophisticated business users everywhere are using mashups to improve collaboration and productivity, providing faster, easier, and more flexible access to business data, promoting employee self-sufficiency, and wringing more ROI value from their data. Forrester Research predicts that mashups that integrate disparate data, add context to the marriage of two data streams, or merge not only data but business processes, will be adopted by the enterprise in a big way—to the tune of a $700 million market by 2013.

Poster Boy

The artist's street name is Poster Boy and his canvases are the advertising billboards that line New York's subway stations. Working minimally with a fifty-cent blade and paste, Poster Boy (vandalism being illegal, he hides his true identity) appropriates advertising imagery—for movies, fancy watches, luxurious liquor—to create subversive art and political collages. Using the MTA stations as his gallery space, Poster Boy is part of a wave of media manipulators, with names like Violator of the Regime and the Decapitator, who turn advertising into guerrilla art with a social statement.

In a world of mere "mustache" miscreants and balloon bandits, Poster Boy goes beyond merely defacing the posters; he mashes numerous images and text lines to create something new. For example, he transformed the logo for the action movie *Iron Man* into IRAN=NAM, and altered a New York Police Department recruitment poster to read MY NYPD KILLED SEAN BELL (the young African American accidently shot to death by police on his wedding day in 2006). A promotion for the NBC show *HEROES* is transformed into the antimedia screed WHORES.

Working stealthily between train arrivals, Poster Boy described his process to *New York* magazine this way: "While the train's here, I scope," he says. "Once it pulls out, I start cutting."

"It takes between one and three posters to create a piece. On average it takes about two minutes to make a piece. The complex compositions can take about 10–15 minutes. Background and foreground colors, font/scale of text, logos, size and position of characters, etc., are all things I consider when combining posters. I try not to think too hard in order to keep it as spontaneous as possible.

"The mash-ups should serve as a lesson to people: artists don't create art, the viewers do," he declared.

Monster Mash

Everywhere you look old product categories are crumbling because merchandisers can no longer aggregate consumers or predict customer tastes the way they once could in the mass media age. The mashup metaphor is having a wider influence throughout the retailing world. Just as the new consumers and their new social swarms expect a Read/Write relationship with the content they consume, they demand customized, personalized, short-run products from change-on-the fly manufacturers. And consumers know—with certainty—that they can get manufacturers to respond to their whims. Looking beyond the Web, we see growing examples of mashups in the marketplace.

In the music business, recording artists like TV on the Radio and Gym Class Heroes that blend rock and hip-hop and soul are part of a wave of performers the industry attempts to categorize as "post-racial" or "afropolitan" largely because they defy any other existing categories. These acts not only reflect the gestalt of the times, they represent the mainstreaming of DIY and indie music forms—from emo to crunk—that once lived on the commercial fringes.

But there is more to the evolving music scene than acts that defy categories—music customers are mashing up the way they buy songs. Historically, music was purchased in album form, a collection of songs organized by the artist reflective of a broader message or theme. While singles—those 45 rpms that the hardware makers endorsed—were ever present, it was album sales that defined the recorded music business.

According to the authority on all things music, *Billboard* magazine, record album sales started to spike in the late 1950s and early 1960s with the success of releases by artists such as Elvis Presley and Frank Sinatra. The arrival of the Beatles in 1964, and the popularity of other chart leaders such as the Monkees and Herb Alpert & the Tijuana Brass, caused album sales to skyrocket. Multimillion-selling albums became commonplace.

And albums remained the consumer configuration of choice throughout the 1970s, 1980s, and 1990s. Albums like Carole King's *Tapestry*, Fleetwood Mac's *Rumours*, and Michael Jackson's *Thriller* became staples in any music collection.

Album sales hit their peak around 2000. The number one album of the year surpassed the 7 million mark in sales in seven of the ten years between 1995 and 2004. The biggest winner of all was *NSYNC's *No Strings Attached*, which sold 9,936,000 copies in 2000.

But things have changed. Unit sales of the year's number one album have declined every year since 2004. The top seller in 2008, Lil Wayne's *Tha Carter III,* sold just 2.88 million units—the lowest sales of a number one album since Nielsen/SoundScan took over tracking of record sales for *Billboard* magazine in 1991.

What is happening? The answer is that consumers have come to prefer buying their music à la carte. While album sales continue to decline, song sales downloaded to devices like the iPod and other MP3s are exploding.

The top two hundred songs for 2008 sold a combined total of 1.07 billion downloads, while the albums for the year sold a combined total of 428.4 million copies. Single songs now outsell albums by a margin of more than two to one.

We can look at the grocery shelves to see more hybrid effects of mashed-up thinking. A walk down the breakfast aisle of any supermarket will find major brands mashing themselves. Consider Pop-Tarts Splitz—the popular toaster pastry that is literally split down the middle, combining strawberry and blueberry, chocolate and vanilla. And a few feet away, the new mashed-up breakfast cereal "ChocoNilla" Cocoa Krispies.

Around the corner, the snack foods shelves are also undergoing a mash revolution. Doritos tortilla chips have been a "macrosnack" category leader since their introduction in 1964. More than most, Frito-Lay has kept a close ear to the changing desires of its consumers and has tapped into the swarm mindset in several important ways. In 2007, the company peered into friendly swarms and asked fans to "Fight for the Flavor," that is, decide which new flavor of snack chip should become a permanent part of its lineup. The follow-up promotion, "The X-13D Flavor Experiment," challenged consumers to name a new product under development.

Then in 2008, the company issued its own versions of mashups with its "Collision" line of chips—single packages featuring different flavor combinations; hot wings and blue cheese, zesty tacos and chipotle ranch. Whether these strategies will ultimately prove successful, Frito-Lay's willingness to experiment, bring consumers to the table early, and even risk brand confusion by mashing its flagship products speaks volumes about how a master marketer sees the landscape shifting.

Fitting In

The word *customer* is a derivative of "custom," meaning "habit"; a customer was someone who frequented a particular shop, who made it a habit to purchase goods there, and with whom the shopkeeper maintained the expectation of an ongoing relationship. By that definition, customers—repeat buyers one can get to know well—are becoming harder to keep every day. Not only is loyalty harder to win, the typical shopper has so many choices and so many competing claims to attention that it is nearly impossible to form habitual shopping patterns.

In their look at the unintended consequences of digital interactivity on markets, John A. Deighton and Leora Kornfeld note that "words like 'viewer' and 'listener,' and others bequeathed to us by the era of centrally-managed media, are limiting. Indeed, the word 'consumer' is of limited value in understanding the new context. The marketer needs to be alert to many roles that are played by the person who lives on the buying side of the buyer-seller dyad, because as marketing becomes more ubiquitous it encounters this person in roles that have nothing to do with consuming or being part of an audience or a market target."

Deighton and Kornfeld advise a new way to see the relationship between maker and buyer in an age of empowered consumers self-organized into close-knit social communities. "The marketer in peer-to-peer environments is an interloper, more talked-about than talking. At best its role is to provoke conversations among consumers, and at worst it becomes the enemy, attacked with invective or parody. Marketing may be less a matter of domination and control, and more a matter of fitting in."

CHAPTER 6

ABUNDANCE COSTS

The High Price of Power

> The road of excess leads to the palace of wisdom.
> —WILLIAM BLAKE

Draeger's Market in Menlo Park, California, is the kind of super-market foodies love. The store carries aisle after aisle of hard-to-find gourmet items not found at the typical Safeway, Ralphs, or Market Basket. Great care is taken with produce, and the staff is quick to help you with a question about product usage or reci-pes. In short, Draeger's was a perfect place to test consumer at-titudes toward choice.

Two researchers, Dr. Sheena S. Iyengar, an assistant professor at Columbia's business school, and Dr. Mark R. Lepper, chair-man of Stanford's psychology department, set out to validate a hypothesis about the positive value of choice in the decision-making process. They figured—as anyone might—that consum-ers would respond positively to more choices—the more the merrier—and they wanted data to prove it.

To do this they set up two sample tables of exotic English jams from Wilkin & Sons. On one table, thirty varieties of jams and jellies. On the other, only six. Of 260 shoppers they encountered that day, nearly 60 percent would congregate around the table with thirty varieties, while only 40 percent gravitated to the table with only six choices. People were clearly attracted to more choices.

However, when the time came to make an actual decision, only 3 percent purchased from among those who viewed the table with thirty choices while 30 percent of those viewing the more limited six choices bought a product. In an apparent paradox, providing fewer choices yielded ten times the sales. After validating their findings with another study of Godiva chocolates, Iyengar and Lepper came up with a simple explanation: shoppers faced "choice overload."

In their article published in the *Journal of Personality and Social Psychology*, Dr. Lepper concluded that "one can go too far in the process of offering choices, and when we are confronted with an array of choices that is larger than we can manage, it has negative effects."

"SKUdzu"

In 1978, during its fourth season, *Saturday Night Live* first aired a recurring skit called "The Scotch Boutique" about a mall store that sold nothing but different types of adhesive tape.

Decades ahead of its time, the prescient sketch lampooned both mall culture and the inanity of highly specialized stores that were then just starting to populate the mall scene. Much of the gag revolved around the lack of business in the mall; the big laughs came from Gilda Radner. As the wife of the shop owner, she observes that, unlike other stores in the center, the Scotch Boutique was doing a booming business because owners of other stores needed to buy tape to put up their "Going Out of Business" signs.

Fast-forward three decades and we find a world filled with Scotch Boutiques.

Thanks to breakthroughs in manufacturing and distribution, supply chain management and mass customization, the Internet and the Long Tail, consumers have experienced an explosion of choices in the past few decades. The clearest view to the proliferation of choice is the explosion of SKUs—the standard stock-keeping units used by manufacturers and retailers to keep track of all the new stuff to sell. SKUs, which provide a unique identifier for each distinct product and service that can be ordered from a supplier, have multiplied by a staggering 500 percent since 1990. Today, there are one million consumer products SKUs on retail shelves.

According to the consulting group A.T. Kearney, "The SKU proliferation problem began decades ago as consumer products companies—electronics, food, cosmetics—answered the siren songs of the era: Get close to the consumer, use target marketing to respond to their every need, and fill shelves with enough choices so not to miss anyone. It has been a drive to innovate—or pseudo-innovate—based on what consumers want or what research says they want."

The result of this single-minded focus?

In *The Paradox of Choice*, Swarthmore College professor and author Barry Schwartz observed that the average American supermarket today carries 285 varieties of cookies, 85 flavors and brands of juices, and 95 varieties of chips. Customers now face 230 soup offerings, 120 different pasta sauces, 275 varieties of cereal, 250 different varieties of mustard, 75 different varieties of olive oil, more than 300 varieties of jam, and 175 different types of tea bags. London-based market research group Datamonitor found that, overall, supermarkets carry more than 45,000 items, with 20,000 new products introduced each year (while the average shopping cart can contain 45 to 50 items—or one item for every 1,000 available). Online, Amazon gives every consumer a bookstore with two million titles, while Netflix promises 35,000 different movies on DVD.

According to retail consultant Art Van Bodegraven, "Every time we, as consumers, turn around, there is another wave of brand extensions to sort through and select from. New flavors, new scents (including scentless), new colors, new sizes, new packaging, new deals. And, when one manufacturer ventures into 'new' territory, the competition is sure to follow, often trying to go the pioneer one better."

The Shopper's Dilemma

According to traditional economic thinking, human beings are rational creatures who, when faced with a choice, weigh the costs and benefits of each option and pick the best among them. It stands to reason, the theory goes, that the more options people are given, the more satisfied they will be. However, we have come to learn that this is not necessarily the case. Abundance, it seems, is not a panacea.

"Such an environment does not fit with our biological heritage, which is one forged amidst scarcity and deprivation," says neuroscientist Peter C. Whybrow of the newfound abundance. Whybrow argues that the human brain is ill equipped to deal with the ready availability of everything we want. In fact, he says, from way back we were designed instead for scarcity. "Physiologically, man is designed to handle poverty. In previous eras, man had to run for his dinner. If he didn't catch it, he didn't eat. While well equipped to deal with scarcity, humans are less well-equipped to deal with abundance."

"The presumption is, self-determination is a good thing and choice is essential to self-determination," says Barry Schwartz.

"But there's a point where all of this choice starts to be not only unproductive, but counterproductive—a source of pain, regret, worry about missed opportunities and unrealistically high expectations."

According to researchers, the human mind is not equipped to evaluate an infinite number of choices and, worse, it is wired to feel regret when we think about the alternatives we've forgone.

Schwartz concludes that "some choice is better than none, but more choice is not always better than less."

And there is a psychic cost to all this freedom of choice. Virginia Postrel, author of *The Future and Its Enemies*, writes, "We're increasingly unhappy, riddled with anxiety and regret, because we have so much freedom to decide what to do with our money and our lives. Some choice may be good, but we've gone over the limit."

There is mounting evidence that consumers are recoiling from the choice conundrum by both limiting situations that require them to choose (or going with products that are simpler and less confusing) and relying on the advice and consent of a narrow group of trusted voices from their social nodes. According to Lepper, "consumer research suggests that as both the number of options and the information about options increases, people tend to consider fewer choices and to process a smaller fraction of the overall information available regarding their choices."

How Wii Won the War

For its fiscal quarter ending November 2007, Nintendo announced it had shipped a U.S. record 981,000 units of its Wii game console. In November 2008, despite a difficult economy,

Nintendo announced it had shattered that record, selling more than two million consoles in the previous quarter—and in the process cementing its lead over Microsoft and Sony in the highly competitive game market. One reason for Nintendo's dominance: simplicity.

First, consider the approach taken by Nintendo's competitors.

With the launch of the Xbox 360 in 2005, Microsoft released two versions of the console: Core and Premium. The Core was considered the "entry point" version, and for $299, consumers had to sacrifice the hard drive, the wireless controller, and a video cable. The Premium version, priced at $399, came with a 20GB hard drive, a wireless controller, and a component (HD) cable. Predictably, the Core model was mostly ignored in favor of the more sensible Premium edition.

Then, Microsoft discontinued the Core model, replacing it with a similar Arcade edition. Priced at $279, the new model again skipped the hard drive, but offered a 256MB memory card and a wireless controller. Next, the company confused the market further with the Xbox 360 Elite, which at $449 was a Premium model dressed up with a black case, an HDMI port, and a bigger hard drive. Finally, in response to the popularity of its Halo game series, Microsoft then introduced a special Halo-themed version of the Premium edition, timed with the release of Halo 3, bringing to five the different versions of the Xbox 360 available to consumers in just two years.

For its part, Sony initially introduced the PS3 with two options: 20GB and 60GB. Consumers didn't see enough difference between the two, so Sony quickly phased out the low-end version only weeks after launch. The lack of a low-end model led Sony to drop the price of the 60GB version and introduce an 80GB version as the high-end PS3. To complicate matters, Sony canceled the 60GB version in favor of a new "low-end" 40GB model.

While its competitors released a variety of system versions and options, Nintendo issued but a single version of its Wii games console. The simplicity of its play connected with consumers, propelling Nintendo from the number three spot to solid category leadership in a year. According to Chris Morell at Game-Pro: "The Wii is leading the videogame hardware market with one console SKU: when you buy a Wii, you buy a Wii, period. Consumers *understand* the Wii, and more importantly, so do parents and older adults, two groups that are propelling Nintendo's explosive growth in the casual games market. Consumers like choice, but they don't want confusion."

Blissful Ignorance

There was a time when information overload and choice proliferation were wielded by brand managers as switching costs—confusion and product churn made customers afraid to switch for fear of missing something new and better. Perversely, this fear may have been mistaken for customer loyalty. Now, with the emergence of analysis paralysis and the rise of reference purchase, we see customers being driven away by the same complexity.

The arrival of the Internet was hailed as a way to shift more power to the consumers—and indeed, the Internet helps consumers analyze large quantities of product-related information, enables comparison shopping, and ultimately leads to better decision making. But the fact is, the Internet has only added to the information whiteout that frustrates consumers. In short, more power is making consumers less happy.

We can expect a backlash to the choice proliferation. For example, the big new story in European retailing is the discount concept of Germany's Aldi stores. Aldi—and its U.S. counterpart, the Trader Joe's chain—doesn't carry any manufacturer brands, only private labels. It also carries only seven hundred SKUs—compared to Wal-Mart's seventy *thousand* SKUs. And yet the company has nearly twice the profit margins.

As part of its plan to survive the auto industry meltdown, Ford CEO Alan Mulally announced in 2008 that the company would be reducing many of its buyer options. By example, he observed that the Lincoln Navigator offered 128 options on its console alone.

"You know what 128-factorial is—it's a lot of combinations," Mr. Mulally joked at a conference, alluding to the number of designs theoretically resulting from mixing and matching the consumer options. (To be exact: 3.85620482×10 to the 215th power.)

But the Internet has always promised consumer empowerment, particularly as it relates to comparing products and product specifications. Here again, however, we see natural limits on the capacity of consumers to manage the information spew. In what they call the "Blissful Ignorance Effect," researchers at the University of Iowa found that people who have only limited information about a product are actually happier with that product than people who have a lot of information.

The researchers employed three experiments to arrive at their conclusions. In two of the trials, subjects were asked for their opinions as consumers—about chocolate in one and hand lotion in the other. In each experiment, one group was given lots of information about the product, the other group much less. In each instance, the subjects who had little information were more optimistic about either the chocolate or hand lotion than those who had more information.

In the third trial, subjects were given the opportunity to choose a video to watch. They were told one of the movies had received unanimously good reviews from critics, while the other received mixed reviews. Although more of the subjects selected the movie they were told was well received, those who selected the movie believing it had mixed reviews had lower expectations and were actually more optimistic about their choice.

"We found that once people commit to buying or consuming something, there's a kind of wishful thinking that happens and they want to like what they've bought," said assistant professor of marketing Dhananjay Nayakankuppam, who led the trials. "The less you know about a product, the easier it is to engage in wishful thinking. But the more information you have, the harder it is to kid yourself. This can be contrasted with what happens before taking any action when people are trying to be accurate and would prefer getting more information to less."

We are also seeing consumers relying more on the opinions of others to help them choose.

In its October 2007 report, "Online Global Consumer Study," the Nielsen Company presented data collected across forty-seven global markets showing that more than three-quarters of surveyed consumers in every category trusted peer recommendations over and above any other product information source—newspapers, television, brand Web sites, even product opinions posted by fellow customers they didn't know.

We can expect a growing number of social recommendation utilities to emerge, companies like TrustedOpinion, Flixster, Spout, and Friend2Friend that allow members to check their friends' opinions on music, movies, books, restaurants and clubs, and an array of consumer products and services.

Consumers are also retreating behind the gated walls of their social networks. According to Darren Sharp, professor of life and social sciences at Swinburne University of Technology, "Users now navigate through an environment of media overload by turning to trusted social networks and peer communities for advice, recommendations and reviews." Sharp says consumers are increasingly "nestled within their social network on which they rely to filter the inherent information overload associated with an abundance of choice. The social network thrives in an environment of trust in order to maintain the highest quality recommendations, reviews and feedback. Reputation can be won or lost depending on the validity of these insights."

Today's consumers are less likely to try to outdo one another for status than to validate their decisions through the advice and consent of their social circles. Now, keeping up with the Joneses increasingly means checking in with them.

Overwhelming consumers with more choices reflects mass market thinking: make many variations on a theme and hope that one version—one size, color, scent, configuration—connects with enough customers to make it worth the investment. *The future of marketing is giving customers exactly what they want without making them choose.* As we shall see in the next section, that reality requires a whole new view of the relationship between producer and consumer.

PART THREE

MARKETING 3.0

The Rise of Consumer Communities

CHAPTER 7

THE PINK CATALLAXY

The Network Collective

> Every economic era is based on a key abundance and a
> key scarcity.
>
> —GEORGE GILDER

Austrian economist Friedrich Hayek was uncomfortable with
the word *economy*. He felt that the Greek root of the word—
"household management"—implied that economic agents operate on the basis of shared goals (which they clearly do not).

In his 1945 essay "The Use of Knowledge in Society," Hayek
argued that creating a "rational economic order . . . is a problem of the utilization of knowledge which is not given to
anyone in its totality" but instead trades on "dispersed bits of
incomplete and frequently contradictory knowledge which all
the separate individuals possess." Instead of economy, Hayek
preferred the term *catallaxy* for "the order brought about by
the mutual adjustment of many individual economies in a
market."

Hayek derived the word *catallaxy* from the Greek verb *katal-
lasso*, which means not only "to exchange or barter" but also "to
admit into the community" and "to change from enemy into
friend." Three rules of Hayek's view of catallaxy were that

—agents work in their own interest to gain income,

—they subjectively weigh and choose preferred alternatives, and

—they have open access to markets.

For economists, the term *catallaxy* has come to mean the natural order that bubbles up from many independent transactions in a free market.

In many ways, the idea of a catallaxy is an apt way to view the new world inside the Internet: a free-market economy in which millions of self-organized, self-interested entities exchange a rich variety of information, goods, and services; sometimes the entities compete, sometimes they collaborate, often they do both simultaneously. The free interaction of many small players makes it a classic catallaxy; its collectivist, collaborative, "wiki" ways give it a slightly pink hue.

Emerging agents of the new Internet catallaxy are the many small social nodes created every minute around the world. These small communities thrive on the raw material (information, people, goods, and services) they derive from the "soup" of the unstructured, Internet-driven global marketplace. These independent congeries are small, tightly knit, highly discriminating social groups of usually fewer than 150 people. These groups are mutual benefit societies that act on self-interest and self-preservation, defined as much by exclusion as by inclusion. They are self-selecting, self-organizing, self-policing, and self-limiting groups. They resent outside intrusion and interruption. They cope with outside threats and stressors (like too many choices) by closing ranks and looking inward. They are trust and reputation economies, within which social capital is the coin of the realm, and where participation is rewarded, indifference punished.

The rise of these small social structures dramatically changes the business landscape inherited from the Industrial Age. Not only have we come to the end of mass marketing and the age of broadcast, we have entered a new era where marketing is more than a conversation, it is an act of cooperation. In a time when media is diffused and signals are abundant, consumer attention is scarce and acceptance is rare. The solution, as we shall see, is not a technological one, but a social one.

Small Circles of Reciprocity

To paraphrase an observation of de Tocqueville's on America, there seem to be more associations on the Internet than there are people. The dynamic catallaxy that is the emerging Internet makes organic group formation easy, and we are already seeing a rich and diverse collection of communities springing up around the globe. According to Wharton researcher Eric K. Clemons:

> *Humans in all cultures at all times form complex social networks; the term* social network *here means ongoing relations among people that matter to those engaged in the group, either for specific reasons (like fantasy football, cancer support groups, task forces at work) or for more general expressions of mutual solidarity (like families, clans, friends, social clubs). Social networks among individuals who may not be related can be validated and maintained by agreement on objectives, social values, or even by choice of entertainment, such as a group of people who meet for tailgating parties when their professional football team plays home games. Membership in these networks can be relatively permanent (extended families, which endure for lifetimes) or flexible (pregnancy support groups, in which members rotate out after a few months). They involve reciprocal responsibilities and roles that may be altruistic or self-interest based (or a combination of both).*

Every technology creates a culture around it. The printing press, automobile, and television all spawned well-documented worldviews around them. Whether a sense of shared knowledge afforded readers of books and newspapers, or the increased personal freedom and wanderlust created by the age of the automobile, or the common denominator society propagated by TV, technology has always been largely about culture. As we saw in chapter 4, the age of industry brought with it many cultural implications—efficiency, linearity, and consumerism among them. In many ways, we are still wrestling with the remnants of Industrial Age thinking in our institutions, markets, and homes. Appropriately, the Internet has arrived with its cultural touchstones, such as transparency, individual empowerment, and the democratization of information. These new forces are starting to change the way we interact and behave.

The essence of the Internet as we know it is cooperation. The system of linking millions of private and public, academic, business, and government computer networks into a single global network was born of cooperation. The very DNA of the Internet can be seen in the original communications protocols that describe how to exchange data over the network. The Transmission Control Protocol/Internet Protocol (TCP/IP) suite of rules not only defined how Internet computers were to communicate, it created a paradigm that has played out for several decades: the beau ideal of the age of information is sharing. The early Net was populated by academics and researchers who wanted to share knowledge more efficiently. This ideal of reciprocity defined the rules of engagement on the Internet. It should have come as no surprise that people would share music, photos, and movies over the Internet, and these first communities were the progenitors of the social nodes that followed. The rules are simple enough: give at least as much as you take.

So what lies behind this impulse to cooperate and reciprocate online? Again, these are instincts deep-rooted in the human experience. In their book *Why Humans Cooperate*, Natalie Henrich and her coauthors argue that reciprocity is a defensive posture best realized in small groups. They write: "From the perspective of institutional design, cultural evolution should exploit our evolved reciprocal psychology by creating institutions that—among other things—partition cooperation into small, enduring social groups."

The Collective

Ray Krause started the Web Geek Collective with a simple stated vision: "I'd like to see this network develop as a place for people interested (or maybe even passionate) about web design and development to turn to for advice and support from fellow web geeks. While the main focus here is on web stuff and seeing how geeks come in all kinds of shapes, sizes and flavors, I can't help but to invite any and all who want to share."

When asked about his motivations for founding the Collective, Krause says, "I really like the idea of people sharing ideas and working with as few restrictions as possible."

As to his growth ambitions, Krause states, "From my own perspective, online groups tend to center around a core of about 10 to 20 members that are always posting and the rest being casual lurkers and the one-time member sign-up. I think an optimal group would be about 100 members."

Krause's ambitions are typical of the approximately half a million community builders using the Ning platform. Ning cofounder and CEO Gina Bianchini says "that they're authentic, that they revolve around something that people are passionate about, and that they're made up of people committed to that network's purpose and to connecting with others around that purpose."

Internet Immigrants

An October 2008 Forrester consumer poll found that 75 percent of Internet users now participate in some form of online social community, up from 56 percent in 2007. When we speak of social community, most people still think of the large-scale communities—those virtual nations like MySpace, Facebook, QQ, Orkut, and others. Predictably, still rooted in our mass media mindset, we tend to see the scale of these communities as an attractive feature; advertise behind the walls of these communities and you can reach a lot of people all at once. Sure, the large offering of both stronger and weaker ties—more friends and more strangers—on a single platform does present an efficient way to assemble a community, but the sheer numbers can be illusory.

In truth, these places are merely the Internet's version of Ellis Island, embarkation processing centers readying new digital immigrants for full-fledged citizenship. People will typically get their feet wet in these giant social communities, reaching out to a broad audience of contacts and names from the past, then they inevitably prioritize into small circles of much more meaningful contacts. As research shows, even when we don't consciously pare down our contact lists, there is a hidden logic at work that shows the true contours of our real communities.

Daniel Romero, a scientist at the Center for Applied Mathematics at Cornell University, working with HP Labs, found out that when it comes to social communities, there are circles within circles.

In 2008, his team focused on the microblogging network Twitter, where people follow the daily postings of their friends. The researchers analyzed a total of 309,740 users, who on average posted 255 posts, had 85 followers, and followed 80 other people. When they measured actual interaction, Romero's team discovered that even within large public/personal networks there are much smaller networks that truly matter.

According to the authors: "Even when using a very weak definition of 'friend,' we find that Twitter users have a very small number of friends compared to the number of followers and followees they declare. (A friend is defined as anyone who a user has directed a post, or '@username,' to at least twice.) This implies the existence of two different networks: a very dense one made up of followers and followees, and a sparser and simpler network of actual friends. The latter proves to be a more influential network in driving Twitter usage since users with many actual friends tend to post more updates than users with few actual friends."

Getting followers is easy, keeping them hard. Scarcity of attention and the daily rhythms of life and work make people default to interacting with just those few who matter and who reciprocate their attention. Therefore people tend to narrow their circles to a manageable number of relationships. In order to be meaningful, these relationships require frequent communication and reciprocity, and time and cognitive capacity are limiting forces.

"People Like Us"

As we have argued throughout this book, the impulse to group formation runs deep in the human psyche. From our earliest days, we humans have banded together in groups for mutual benefit and protection. Until recently, the choices we had of whom to group with were bounded by the practical limitations of locality and geography. Today we have no such constraints. Thanks to the Internet, we can now form social constructs and compacts with whomever we want regardless of where they live or how we are connected. However, we once formed groups with those closest in bloodlines or geographic proximity; today, the Internet empowers us to form groups completely of our own making.

Marketing analyst J. Walker Smith described the phenomenon as "self-invention," a desire to shape and control our identities and our surroundings. People are unwilling to live with trade-offs, he said. So they are "re-creating their environments to fit what they want in all kinds of ways, and one of the ways is that they are finding communities that fit their values—where they don't have to live with neighbors or community groups that might force them to compromise their principles or their tastes."

Even with our choices we seem to be inventing our worlds, says anthropologist Robert Kozinets: "Consumers are consumers primarily in that they take commercial identities as important aspects of themselves and their collectives; that they use the identity to relate to themselves, to other people and to the world around them. . . ."

Rubicon Web marketing group has developed a taxonomy around five categories of online community:

- ▶ Proximity, where users share a geographic location (Yelp, Judy's Book, Insider Pages);
- ▶ Purpose, where they share a common task (Kiva, Wikipedia, DonorsChoose);
- ▶ Passion, where they share a common interest (Dogster, MyChurch, FanNation);
- ▶ Practice, where they share a common career or field of business (Lawyrs.net, Med3q.com); and
- ▶ Providence, where they discover connections with others (Facebook, LinkedIn).

Purdue University researcher Nicole R. Brown studied the group behaviors inside a community of "passion" called Spread-Net, a community for fans of the popular band Widespread Panic. Her findings showed that the community was both close-knit and discriminating: "Members of SpreadNet are largely homogenous, and such homogenization constructs a stark divide/boundary between those on the inside and those on the outside. In other words, rather than operating as what is commonly thought of as a Web or network, SpreadNet seems to operate as an enclave or silo." Moreover, "access to online technologies can be viewed similarly to gated neighborhoods or universities, secured not only by material means but by ideological and operational means as well."

The One Percent Solution

Duncan Watts, author of *Six Degrees* and now a researcher at Yahoo!, sparked a small firestorm in March 2008 in an interview given to *Fast Company* magazine entitled "Is the Tipping Point Toast?" In the piece, Watts disputes Malcom Gladwell's theory of the *influentials*—those bellwether trendsetters identified in his bestseller *The Tipping Point*.

About the Law of the Few, Gladwell writes that "in a given process or system, some people matter more than others." In other words, reach these elusive, yet highly connected gatekeepers and you can reach the world. Watts disagrees and asserts that businesses are wasting billions of dollars every year targeting these mythical tastemakers who really don't lead trends.

Ultimately, Watts argues, new trends reaching a tipping point have less to do with the person trying to propagate the trend and everything to do with the trend itself. In fact, Watts claims, if a community is already open to embrace a trend, then anyone in the group can kick-start the adoption. On the other hand, if the group is unwilling to adopt the idea—if the culture of a community prevents people from easily getting "infected" with new ideas—then no one has a chance of getting that idea to spread.

The Gladwell-Watts debate points to one of the paradoxes of small online groups: while many groups pride themselves on social equality in all affairs, simply by being more active or vocal, a small minority of members seem to carry more weight than others.

Many studies have shown that both participation in group discussion and influence over final decisions have generally been found to be more equal in electronic groups than in traditional face-to-face groups. And we know that people tend to join groups where they feel an affinity and can be safe as one among equals. So Watts is correct in asserting that small groups of equals cannot be unreasonably persuaded to do something by one of their own—unless they want to in the first place. In fact, there is evidence that ideas that percolate up from the rank and file are often better reflectors of group sentiment and readiness.

However, the truth is that some members tend to be more involved, articulate, and prolific than others, and these people do wield a disproportionate influence if only in that they create more conversations than the rank and file. So Gladwell's Law of the Few also applies in online circles—at least as a function of the power of participation.

In *The Wisdom of Crowds*, author James Surowiecki refers to this power as "talkativeness."

Talkativeness may seem like a curious thing to worry about, but in fact talkativeness has a major impact on the kinds of decisions small groups reach. If you talk a lot in a group, people will tend to think of you as influential almost by default. Talkative people are not necessarily well liked by other members of the group, but they are listened to. And talkativeness feeds on itself. Studies of group dynamics almost always show that the more someone talks, the more he is talked to by others in the group. So people at the center of the group tend to become more important over the course of a discussion. In a market or even a democracy, champions are far less important because of the sheer number of potential decision makers. But in a small group, having a strong advocate for an idea, no matter how good it is, is essential.

In a 2006 paper on influence inside small brand communities, University of Paris researcher Lionel Sitz found that the "hard-core" group members wielded significant influence inside their communities; they are often the organizers of the community, moderators of the forums, or the most active posters and readers in these forums.

Our analysis shows that hard-core members are generally considered to be the most trustworthy members and their advice and opinions are generally well accepted and respected by the other members. The respect for hard-core members is visible through many reverent references to their names and memory as well as the numerous thanks addressed to them by the other members. Less active members are generally less experts in the domain and ask a lot of questions. These questions lead the experts to objectify their experiences, make explicit their relevance in order to share this knowledge. In a sense, there is a status-based division of labor between the members of a brand community.

In online communities, a hidden hierarchy is visible in the categories created by the community to distinguish either the incumbency or activity level of its members (for example, "moderator," "gold member," "newbie"). According to author Suzanne Weisband in the *Academy of Management Journal*, "When groups make decisions, high-status group members often talk more than low-status group members and exert more influence on final outcomes."

Studies of many online social groups and crowdsourcing projects point to a magical "one percent" in any social construct. In any group of one hundred people online, one person will actually create new content, ten people will "interact" with the content (comment or offer improvements), and the other eighty-nine people will just view it. In some cases, the disparity among producers and consumers is even greater. According to the Church of the Customer blog, on Wikipedia 50 percent of all article edits are contributed by 0.7 percent of users, and more than 70 percent of all articles have been written by just 1.8 percent of all users.

A September 2008 report on influence within online communities from Rubicon Consulting showed the following:

▶ *Small groups of enthusiasts dominate most online conversations,* but that doesn't mean online communities matter only to a narrow segment of people. Most Web users read community content rather than contributing to it and are strongly influenced by the things they see there, especially product reviews and recommendations.

▶ *Marketers should view an online discussion in the context of a theater performance* in which the community leader(s) interacts with a small group of contributors while a larger number of people look on. Companies who turn away from communities populated by enthusiasts have mistaken fellow actors for the audience.

The key finding of the report: the most frequent contributors have a strong influence on purchase decisions because they write most of the online recommendations and reviews.

"Many companies downplay the importance of online communities because only a few percent of all Internet users contribute to them heavily," said Harry Max, a principal at Rubicon Consulting. "What they don't understand is that most other Internet users read those reviews and rely on them heavily when making purchase decisions."

In small, self-organized online social groups, where trust and reciprocity are high, all opinions tend to be—on their face—equally influential. Yet we can see that a vocal minority—those who write the most posts, comment more frequently, or spend more time in forums—do gain weighted legitimacy and wield more influence than others. As a practical matter, clearly the trick for marketers is to enlist the most vocal and hard-core members as advocates.

The Eleven People You Will Meet Online

Adrian Chan of the Web design firm Gravity7 has extensively studied the typical personalities that show up in online social communities and has created a useful list of the top eleven types. Each personality profile affords a view to the way communities create their unique cultures and can be instrumental in winning admission to the community. The personality types are: Status Seeker, Critic, Socializer, Emcee, Lurker, Buddy, Creator, Pundit, Rebel, Officiator, and Harmonizer.

The Status Seeker wants recognition and enjoys accumulating symbolic tokens of influence—from the number of friends visibly listed to online badges and awards. For the Status Seeker rank and position is everything and online stats are the measuring sticks that matter. The Status Seeker checks his/her stats regularly and frequently compares his/her stats with others.

The Critic is very interested in the substance and meaning of things. He or she may understand the multiple perspectives on a topic, and appreciate all sides of the relevant arguments, opinions, and positions of others, but usually likes to point out the finer distinctions between the views. The Critic may frequently edit and update content as much to eliminate inaccuracies as to keep information current and will believe that audience approval is a measure of his/her understanding, intelligence, accuracy, and insight—not popularity, attractiveness, performance, or even originality.

The Socializer believes deeply in the power of online communities and derives a sense of well-being from online interactions. Goes online for information about friends, events, games, and social news, keeps track of what his/her friends are up to, and goes online to "stay in the loop." The Socializer makes new friends and contacts easily, and creates friendly contributions and content—testimonials, notes, and comments. Socializers pay attention when invited into a conversation and like to keep one eye online even when busy elsewhere.

The Emcee is a performer at heart, and works to make an impression as well as engages the audience by means of wit, personality, and character: personality. The Emcee pays attention to attention and can be more interested in social validation, drawing attention, and capturing an audience than in community content itself—behavior that may rankle some group purists.

The Lurker is self-effacing in his/her presence online and has obvious concerns about privacy, security, safety, and authenticity. Paradoxically, the Lurker tends to be a very active community participant, logging in consistently, creating site visits, traffic, and page views by browsing. This type is often an observant participant, and may eventually serve as a resource to those who spend a lot of time online.

The Buddy has a strong sense of friendship and values companionship and is likely to flirt, play, tease, and joke with friends online. In addition to spending time with friends online, and in online activities, has clear ideas of loyalty, friendship, inner trust circles and the expectations that accompany them. The Buddy is familiar with the language and rituals of community, including ways of talking, insider jokes, and is acutely aware of what friends think of him/her, takes notice of the presence or absence of friends online, and will do what friends do.

The Creator sees the online community as a creative medium and actively creates, builds, makes, publishes. The Creator provides the bulk of content that others share, pass around, rate, vote, and comment on— the kind of user-generated content that makes sites and services successful. This type is of significant value in re-contextualizing and interpreting community culture within the group.

The Pundit considers him- or herself a topic leader or expert, and routinely offers the latest news, opinions, and observations. This type is personally interested in playing the part of news anchor and industry commentator even if not deeply interested in making news him- or herself. The Pundit may believe that he or she has a reputation, an audience or following, and may regularly talk to his or her audience in order to maintain it. Often serves as an authority members look to to validate or dispute claims made by others.

The Rebel can be a frequent heckler given to subverting the order or upsetting the majority—but not so much as to be shunned. A fixture of "hacker" culture, the Rebel may disrupt online chats and discussions for the sake of attention, may be cynical and work to undermine those who take the community too seriously; inclined to disrupt commercial activities, push an agenda, or game the system.

The Officiator is a stickler for rules, conventions, characters, positions, or roles, and knows how a situation should go. The Officiator believes in order online and the value of convention, normative rules, obligations, and expectations and may proactively embody and play the role for the sake of the system, game, or situation. Likely to take an interest in the rituals, ceremonies, and "trappings" of online communities: tokens, points, leaderboards, ranking, game events. This type believes in collaboration and cooperation, and may presume that cooperation is a universally shared belief for the reason that his or her notion of society requires that it applies equally and to all.

The Harmonizer appreciates group membership and a sense of belonging, but unlike the Emcee, this personality type is motivated by the group's relationships and not its value as an audience. The Harmonizer gives good attention to others, is socially sensitive and responsive, and may triangulate or mediate group interactions. Pays attention to the debts and obligations among members of a group (who is affected by whom) and is mindful of how group members are doing and checks in with friends and colleagues when they fade or drift away from the group.

The New Marketing Logic

In their 2004 article "Evolving to a New Dominant Logic for Marketing," authors Stephen L. Vargo and Robert F. Lusch write that marketing is transitioning from the simple exchange of goods toward service, interactivity, connectivity, and ongoing relationships. As we assert throughout this book, this new model is conducted within the growing number of tightly knit social circles provided by online media. Advertising executive Chuck Brymer calls these private communities *swarms*. "The human swarm phenomenon is fundamentally changing marketing, because instead of just relying on authority figures, 'expert sources,' mainstream media and mass advertising, people are relying on members of their own swarm—such as friends, family, peers, and fellow online community members—to guide their decisions," Brymer argues.

Validating this viewpoint, a November 2008 nationwide survey from e-commerce software maker Guidance showed that nearly 30 percent of online shoppers say the best way to find discounts online is through link forwarding, peer comments, or social sites.

According to Wharton researcher Clemons: "Social networks are trusted because of shared experiences and the perception of shared values or shared needs. A professor is likely to request recommendations for an accountant from another professor, assuming that their requirements are similar and that a colleague's recommendation will be both relevant to his needs and trustworthy. New parents will get recommendations from their neighbors for a pediatrician and, over time, will get recommendations for a baby sitter. Friends tell friends about restaurants and movies."

Ning's Gina Bianchini agrees: "In a world enabled by a map of interests and passions, not only will you meet people who share your interests and passions, but you will also discover brands that want to connect with you *because* of your interests and passions. This cracks the code on monetizing social networks that doesn't exist on any other platform: connecting brands to people who are *self-identified* as having a specific interest or passion *in the context* of that interest or passion. Zombie lovers at Lost Zombies are going to be psyched to hear about the latest horror movie from a big studio. The members of Brand Tampa are going to be excited to hear about a new direct flight out of Tampa to Chicago."

War of the (Small) Worlds

In Neal Stephenson's novel *The Diamond Age*, readers are taken to a far-future Shanghai at a time when nations have been replaced by enclaves of common cultures called "claves." In this balkanized world of ethnic and economic ghettoes, there is much tension and paranoia between the residents of the claves; each community defines itself by who is kept out as much as by who is allowed in.

The more connected we get the more divided we become.

From the beginning the Internet has evoked both darkly dystopian ideas as well as cheerfully utopian visions. Today, we see another duality: the emergence of a giant connected global milieu populated by millions of closely knit social nodes. We should acknowledge that there is a downside risk to the formation of many small segregated and closed communities—online and off. As we have noted, communities are forged and hewn by both common interests and common threats. Members of small social groups find identity in being the same and different at the same time. This opens the possibilities for new ways to divide humankind into factions; the need to side ourselves with and against others is as old as the species.

Virtual reality pioneer Jaron Lanier recently set off an Internet firestorm when he began to criticize the wiki phenomenon. From his essay in *Time* magazine:

> *People have often been willing to give up personal identity and join into a collective. Historically, that propensity has usually been very bad news. Collectives tend to be mean, to designate official enemies, to be violent, and to discourage creative, rigorous thought. Fascists, communists, religious cults, criminal "families"—there has been no end to the varieties of human collectives, but it seems to me that these examples have quite a*

lot in common. What's to stop an online mass of anonymous but connected people from suddenly turning into a mean mob, just like masses of people have time and time again in the history of every human culture?

The rise of new online social constructs holds the hope of new forms of community; self-organized, self-determined social circles can provide a positive means to cope with a chaotic world of abundant information and nearly unlimited choice. But we must be mindful of our ancient impulse to turn our differences—political, ideological, religious—into divisions and rancor. While there is every reason to hope that this unique catallaxy we call the Internet can foster a new era of understanding and intimacy, we can never forget the deep-seated potential for humans to fear what we are not and hate what we don't understand.

CHAPTER 8

THE SELFISH MEME

From Mass Media to Mass Connections

All mass movements avail themselves of action as a
means of unification.
                              —ERIC HOFFER

When in 1976 Richard Dawkins introduced the idea of the
"meme" in his landmark book *The Selfish Gene,* he helped explain
how common experience and culture is created inside mass societies. He defined a meme as a self-replicating information arti-
fact, something held in one individual's memory, which is capable
of being copied to another individual's memory. This includes
anything that can be learned or remembered: ideas, knowledge,
habits, beliefs, skills, images, slogans, and sayings. A meme was
a perfect way to describe the diffusion of ideas through mass
media: simple, easy-to-recall catchphrases and images that a
broad audience might willingly—even unthinkingly—internalize,
celebrate, and pass along. The problem is we no longer live in a
mass-media reality and it is exceedingly difficult today to introduce a meme into the mainstream (whatever that is).

Take the case of the venerable chain letter.

Anyone with e-mail (or a postal address for that matter) has
inevitably received a message promising good luck if it is forwarded on to others—and terrible misfortune if it isn't. Given

our overflowing in-boxes and brimming bulk mail folders, the array of such forwarded missives has exploded in recent years with the widespread adoption of e-mail and social media. The question is, what motivates people in online social circles to pass information—news, gossip, rumors, special offers, coupons, chain letters—on to other people they know? Moreover, why do they send to some friends and associates and not to others? What can marketers do to learn from and tap into these impulses?

In March 2008 two researchers, Jon Kleinberg of Cornell University and David Liben-Nowell of Carleton College, set out to answer some of these questions in a study they conducted of two online petitions that began circulating during the past decade. What they found surprised many experts who thought they understood viral marketing: people are not random but rather highly discriminate in their word-of-mouth communications.

One of the online petitions Kleinberg and Liben-Nowell looked at was in support of National Public Radio and began circulating in 1995; the other was in opposition to the U.S. invasion of Iraq, and originated in 2002. The messages had the common characteristic of being widely disseminated—the researchers found 316 copies of the public radio petition containing more than 13,000 signatures, and 637 copies of the Iraq petition with nearly 20,000 signatures.

Based on this data, the two researchers mapped out how these messages traveled from recipient to recipient on a tree diagram. Analysis of the diagram challenges the common assumptions about how messages spread through social networks, including the holy grail of online marketing: viral contagion theory. Rather than spreading wildly like a virus, with each message producing many direct "descendents" in the tree diagram, the data suggest that people are selective in forwarding messages to others in their social networks. In fact, Kleinberg and Liben-Nowell discovered that 90 percent of the time, forwarded messages produced only a single descendent. That means only 10 percent of the time did a recipient pass along the petition to more than one person at a time.

Kleinberg and Liben-Nowell's research suggests that online messages travel in a less profligate, more considered pattern than was previously assumed. It also means that messages can spread through some groups of people very quickly and take a relatively longer period of time to reach others, creating opportunities for the original message to be abbreviated or changed. "All of this adds up," Kleinberg says, "to cause a much more complex picture of how this information flows though social networks."

So now that we know that people don't pass along information unless they have a reason to do so, the reasonable next question is: what reasons do we need?

Answering that question is not simple; it starts with an understanding of basic human motivations, both intrinsic and extrinsic. According to anthropologist Robert Kozinets, "Intrinsic motivation is a person's sense that they are doing something because they want to do it, because the doing brings joy, it is rewarding by itself, on its own as an activity. Extrinsic rewards suggest that there is actually an instrumental relationship at work, that you do the activity in order to get something else, and that something else (like a monthly check) is actually the reward for doing it."

So one view is that people, being rational beings, do things because they receive psychic, social, or material rewards for doing them. Bottom line: you can't compel someone to spread the word, only induce or reward them to do so.

The classic study of spreading the word—rumor-mongering—was done in 1948 by Gordon Allport and Leo Postman and captured in their book *The Psychology of Rumor*. The most compelling assertion by the pair was that there is a "basic law of rumor" at work. Their "law" states that rumor strength will vary with the importance of the subject to the individual, multiplied by the ambiguity of the evidence pertaining to the topic at hand, expressed as $R = i \times a$. This formula was not intended to be scientific, but does get us to recognize the idea of "importance" to the spread of a rumor. In effect, we need to know why someone might think certain information was worth the time and effort to pass along.

Many follow-on researchers have developed a view that rumor-mongering is a form of collective problem-solving. In other words, people spread rumors in the hope that the group will take action on a matter. For those people who place the norms of the group above all, that makes rumor spreading a beneficial, even noble, act in service of the group interest.

But that doesn't explain why we send to some people and not to others. In order to understand these motivations, we need to know a little about the concept of "moral hazard."

In 1993, Jonathan Frenzen and Kent Nakamoto conducted a comprehensive study to examine what conditions had to be met before a message would be widely passed along. Their study looked at a number of factors, including the nature of the message itself, and the concept of moral hazard—or how sending it would negatively impact the messenger. For the test, they used news about a store sale. In one social network, they studied how fast word would spread about a 20 percent off sale. In another social network, they used a sale where the discounts were deeper—50 to 70 percent off. In a third set of scenarios, they introduced a moral hazard variable by making quantities either very limited or practically unlimited.

What they found was quite telling. When the offer wasn't that remarkable (only 20 percent off), the word of mouth was kept inside a relatively small subset of strong ties. The information was simply not noteworthy or valuable enough to go out of one's way to mention to mere acquaintances. The senders chose not to expend social capital for a mediocre offer.

On the other hand, news of the deeper discounts was widely and quickly passed around to a broader universe of recipients. Perceiving that the offer would be welcomed by the recipient, the senders were eager to share the news. This is consistent with human nature: we believe it elevates our social status within our circles to be the first to tell someone about something remarkable. People will go out of their way to share this, spreading the word far and wide, across strong ties and weak ties alike.

Similarly, in the scenario where the quantity of sale items was unlimited, the pass-around effect was profligate: people were generous in spreading the word about something both they and their friends and associates could benefit from equally. Where things got complicated was in the moral hazard raised by scarcity.

When the offer was deeply discounted but limited to small supply, the news was not widely passed around, and in fact might not be passed along at all. What explains this phenomenon? Again, human nature: if we tell too many people, we ourselves might not get a chance to take advantage of the limited supply of sale items. In such a case, chances are, we won't tell anyone until we have availed ourselves of the deal first, and even then, we'll probably only tell those we're closest to.

So the lesson for marketers is that the information we want to spread needs to be important enough for a transmitter to expend social capital in order to send but not so valuable that it demotivates and conflicts the sender with issues of self-interest.

The latest thinking about rumor-spreading—indeed all word-of-mouth communications—is that such transactions must be two-way. In other words, there must be a reward for both the sender and the receiver in the exchange.

The "Friend" Medium

"We're trying to make ads suck less in social networks," says Seth Goldstein, founder of San Francisco–based SocialMedia Networks.

In 2008, Goldstein's company launched a service called Friend-Rank that analyzes who your best friends are, ranks them according to their nearness to you, then turns you or your friends into the hook of a marketing message. The FriendRank algorithm studies how people interact with Facebook and MySpace apps—those thousands of widgets that can be embedded in a user's profile—to determine who, among someone's hundred or so friends, is most important to them. The program looks at frequency and volume of communications, and activities like game-playing, to determine who among a wide universe of "friends" is actually a part of someone's inner circle.

For example, instead of a generic banner advertising a newly released movie, a social banner might ask you which of your close friends, among a short list, you'd like to invite to see the movie. Or, a social banner might inform you that a friend just gave the movie three stars and ask you to "click here to buy tickets at Fandango."

Goldstein says that the response rate to standard display advertising on social networks is abysmal. People click on ads only about 0.02 percent of the time. By comparison, Goldstein says, early tests of FriendRank show that people are two hundred times more likely to respond to a social ad featuring an endorsement from a friend.

The FriendRank scheme is not the first (and clearly not the last) effort to monetize friendship connections. A problem is that such manipulations raise privacy concerns among consumers. In 2007, Facebook suffered a high-profile PR disaster with the brief launch of its Beacon program. Working with sites like eBay and Yelp, Beacon would automatically alert friends when someone in their circle performed an action—such as buying a product, or making a restaurant reservation. After Facebook members reacted badly, the company backed off and made the program entirely opt-in for members.

The next wave of friend-based ads may be even more sophisticated. Instead of merely co-opting your friends as tacit endorsers, the next models may well incentivize your friends to sell you. *In other words, find the influencer in a group of friends, and pay him/her to place ads on their profile.*

In 2006 Tom coined the term *beme* for the type of incentivized communications that might be propelled friend to friend. Paying homage to Dawkins's *meme* of thirty years earlier and recognizing that the message requires active participation, a beme is a device that rewards both sender and receiver for the exchange. By example, an offer that provides a deep discount on a product might only be activated for the sender when the message is opened by a receiver. The sender has good reason to pass along the offer, and there is a prize for the recipient to take the exchange. A good example of a beme campaign was the Subservient Chicken promotion launched by Burger King in 2004. Under the banner of "Get chicken the way you like it," the online campaign drove viewers to a site that allowed them to interact with an actor absurdly dressed in a chicken suit and lingerie. The link to the site was eagerly passed along from friend to friend because there was a perceived psychic reward for both sender and recipient. Moreover, the stunt worked because Burger King did not seem to overtly push the site: the Chicken got more than a million hits in its first twenty-four hours and is still going strong.

The Secret Language of Social Groups

These studies shed light on personal motivations, but as we have seen in earlier chapters every social group creates its own unique culture, including rules, spoken and unspoken, about how "meaningful" information can and should be passed along.

Meaning itself is a social phenomenon, produced not by individuals for themselves, but by groups, communities, societies, and cultures that maintain—through language and agreed understandings—certain shared knowledge and common touchstones. All groups, communities, societies, and cultures preserve collections of narrative meaning through their myths, fairy tales, legends, histories, and stories. To fully participate requires a general knowledge of these accumulated narratives and histories. And since the cultural stock of meaning is always in flux—new ways of seeing the world are always being created by members while older ideas fade due to lack of use—being in tune with a community requires diligence and active participation.

Although group culture is complex, you can get a general idea of a small group's character by studying some key cultural indicators common to tightly knit communities:

Vocabulary. Every group adopts is own lexicon, attitude, and tone. By studying the community's shared vocabulary it is possible to determine who is part of the group, who isn't, who is new to the group, and who the veterans are.

Rituals. Groups naturally develop rituals—customs, ceremonies, daily activities, and regular features that mark particular occasions. For example, groups may mark member birthdays or holidays in a unique way, or routinely gather to comment on external events.

1. *Practices*. Each group has a way of doing things, even protocols for addressing each other and resolving conflicts.
2. *Stories*. In their discussions and comments group members use narratives to tell about the group. Stories usually convey the group's values, priorities, power distribution, and member relationships. Stories often have a moral or message, although the moral may not be explicit. Stories told to newcomers let the rookies know how group members are supposed to behave.
3. *Shorthand*. Like language, established groups frequently use jargon, acronyms, and other communications shortcuts that deepen the sense of group unity by confusing outsiders and newbies.
4. *Sacred Objects*. Brands and other nonverbal symbols represent key aspects of the group. Logos or emblems are good examples of objects that reflect the culture of a group.

Anthropologists use the term *communitas* to describe the intimacy that exists between people who are connected to each other. In a sense, true community has always been less about bricks and mortar or online infrastructure and more about the emotional and psychological bonds between people with a shared affinity, sense of purpose, and perhaps joined destiny.

In his book *The Virtual Community*, Howard Rheingold made the concept of the online community popular, defining virtual communities as "social aggregations that emerge from the Net when enough people carry on those public discussions long enough, with sufficient human feeling, to form webs of personal relationship in cyberspace." Rheingold argued that it was the interactions between users that provided the proof that community existed, not the need for a physical locus.

As sociologist Barry Wellman puts it, in the future "the person, not the place, household, or workgroup . . . will become even more of an autonomous communication mode." In other words, it is the ties that bind that make a community and now those human connections are actually a form of medium. We are no longer reliant on television, radio, or any other mass distribution system; we get our news from each other personally delivered and intimately customized.

As we have argued throughout this book, small groups don't operate the same as a mass society. People in small social nodes want to fit in, want to be accepted. They want to be surrounded by like-minded people whose opinion they can trust and whose counsel they can count on. Even the harshest Critic or Rebel wants ultimately to "go along to get along" and is unlikely to break the rules of etiquette that guide the group. Small-group members want the benefits of sociability and camaraderie but don't want a lot of drama.

Any successful marketing effort must account for the special bonds and secret language of the group or risk being rejected or even reviled. Moreover, we have made the case in the preceding chapters that people behave differently in groups than they do when acting alone. That goes for their behavior as consumers as well. In fact, collective consumer behavior usually produces results not possible when individuals think and act alone. This dynamically and radically changes the nature of modern commerce: we have come to the end of mass marketing driven by mass communications and its resulting mass culture. As blogger Brian Clark eloquently puts it, "Mass media is a historical aberration. For a short 70-odd years of human history, a relatively small group of people told us what to think and what to buy, and we were expected to passively accept it. That's not how things worked for thousands of years before, and that's not how it's going to work in the future. Clinging to the precepts of a brief period of weirdness may not be the best model to guide us."

Bottom line: the one-way broadcast, mass media consciousness of the past century is rapidly being replaced by a mass-connected social information space feeding and being fed by millions of small, trust-based social groups. The only way to successfully penetrate these tightly-knit communities is through a throwback form of marketing called handselling. Handselling relies on context—affinity and intimacy—and deeply personalized behavior—trust and permission to make the sale. But as we shall see in the next chapter, marketers will not even get to make their case in these small group communities unless they are first invited in as members.

CHAPTER 9

MARKETING IS MEMBERSHIP

Handselling to a Fragmented World

> The bottom line is that people buy from people, not companies.
>
> —LEE J. COLAN

Let's talk business. Or more precisely: marketing and sales.

The question *How do you sell anything in this new economy?* has been at the heart of this book almost from page one. We assume you are here not just because of curiosity about the emerging global marketplace, but because you want strategies and tactics for running successful enterprises in this new world.

Having read this far, you've seen that almost none of the current rules work. Indeed, many of the most effective sales and marketing *techniques* of today—mass advertising, spam, junk mailers—not only will not work but, in the wrong places, may actually be destructive to the company using them.

By the same token, traditional answers regarding the *scale* of sales and marketing campaigns no longer seem applicable, either. The local retailer, should it stick with traditional local advertising, may find itself blindsided by a new competitor operating from the far side of the world. Conversely, a large multinational concern, indulging itself in the usual expensive mass-market advertising, may now find itself wasting millions on campaigns targeted at small market niches that only respond to intimate, insider pitches.

As if all of that isn't enough, the *content* of most traditional corporate advertising campaigns—hyperbolic, generalized to the largest possible audience, dumbed down to the lowest educational level—may, paradoxically, be both insufficiently generalized *and* too dumbed down for the target audience. It depends upon whether the company has targeted one end of what has become a bipolar marketplace (the fast-moving global mass market) or the other (small, insular microniches). To sit in the middle between both marketplaces, neither fish nor fowl—in other words, to continue to use traditional marketing and sales tools—is to court disaster.

So, when we speak of doing business in the new global marketplace, we are really talking about two distinct, and almost mutually exclusive, marketplaces, each with its own personality, rules, internal clock, and system of rewards and punishments. And that, in turn, means that it will be almost impossible for any one company, no matter how large or sophisticated, to pursue both of these markets at the same time.

It may be possible to pursue them sequentially, though that would require a level of adaptability unknown in any major company in the world today (and that may prove to be the driving force behind the adoption of the Protean Corporation model, which we will soon describe). It also may be possible to pursue both markets in parallel—but the two halves of any company that would attempt this would be so distinctly different that they would essentially be two independent companies with few advantages accruing from common systems, operations, or personnel.

What this means is that most companies, at the earliest stages of their histories—probably even on their initial business plans—will have to make a crucial decision that will define everything that follows: will they pursue the global mass market or a constellation of scores, even hundreds, of small microniches?

That may sound odd, but in practice it will be no different from choosing today to be a vertical company or a horizontal one, a company built through internal growth or acquisition, a product company or a service company, a manufacturer or a reseller/distributor/retailer. Most every company makes these decisions today; so adding one more will probably be all but unnoticed—especially as some of the older distinctions become irrelevant.

But whether the decision for the young company to go mass global or "mass local" is made unconsciously or as a separate discussion in the business plan, it will have a defining effect upon the culture and operations of that company from the very first day, which will only deepen as the years pass.

Because these (with apologies to C. P. Snow) "Two Cultures" are so manifestly different, we need to look at each of them—and especially how they deal with their customers—in isolation. We'll begin with the mass global market.

Going Global

Consider the world market for products and services twenty years hence.

The first thing you notice is its sheer *size*: as many as three billion people—half the world's population and representing everyone linked together, via wireless, to the Internet—all clamoring for everything from basic necessities to cosmetics and personal improvement products to luxury items to the very latest fad products. Though there will be the inevitable business cycles, this market will almost always be insatiable for the newest and the hottest, be it consumer electronics, snack foods, or entertainment.

But this global market won't only be about its unprecedented size. There are also two other giant forces at work.

One of these is *speed*. In a wired world—which is what the planet will be by then, covered from pole to pole, from the deepest canyon to the highest peak (and beyond into airplanes flying overhead)—everyone will be able to get on the Web and into the global marketplace *right now*. Indeed, many people once on will almost never get off. And thanks to search engines and increasingly sophisticated tools such as digital "spiders," these multitudes will be able to find the information they need at lightning speeds.

When we think about speed of access, we often forget that it has the secondary effect of accelerating all sorts of other things—including the shortening of attention spans, the abbreviation of product life cycles, and the feeding of an ever-greater thirst for novelty. These three billion consumers are going to know about everything, are going to want everything, and are going to be perpetually bored with everything old and in search of everything new. Needless to say, within this trend lie both opportunities and dangers.

The other giant force is *complexity*. Most of those next two billion consumers are going to join the world economy via simple cell phones, which will limit their ability to fully participate in the global marketplace. But "simple" is a relative term when we're talking about electronics. For example, the processor inside the typical throwaway budget cell phone of the type now flooding the developing world has more computing power than the most powerful mainframe computer of the 1960s. Meanwhile, the display on this cheapo cell phone is able to portray greater detail and complexity than the average desktop computer of the 1980s. And the software and firmware already embedded in the phone the day it arrived is more complex than that which put the Apollo astronauts on the moon.

And Moore's Law guarantees that this rate of change will trail only five to ten years behind the state of the art.

What that means in practice is that the most sophisticated (and expensive) iPhone, BlackBerry, or Nokia phone selling today for $300 or more will be the giveaway-with-a-two-year-service-contract phone handed out by the millions in the Third World in 2020. Now, imagine that adoption curve and multiply it by the number of music and video downloads, ringtones, games, and Web visits associated with them now and you get an idea of just how gigantic this marketplace is going to be.

Meanwhile, keep in mind that today's iPhone or Android phone will just be the *baseline* device for two billion people a decade from now. For the wealthier first billion—and increasingly the millions who join them thanks to the new economy—Moore's Law will have driven Web access technology just that much further ahead. How far? Picture today's most powerful desktop computer in a device the size of a credit card, HD (or perhaps even 3D) displays, Web access speeds in the hundreds of megabytes per second, sophisticated animation and modeling, biometrics, et cetera. These devices will be powerful enough not only to access just about anything in the world instantly, but even to begin to generate a lot of that content itself.

And that's just the phones! Make the comparative leap in performance we see today between mobile phones and laptop computers, and you'll have an idea of the sheer power of those latter devices a decade from now. And we haven't even mentioned all of those embedded Web access devices that will be found everywhere from your car's dashboard to just about every available surface in your home. The consumer in the developed world in 2020 is likely to be within arm's (or voice) reach of a powerful Internet access device twenty-four hours a day. We will literally be enveloped by the Web.

Combine all of that speed and complexity of content—and then empower three billion people with it—and you get an idea of what it will be like to market and sell to the global mass market.

Mass Mass Marketing

Based upon what we already know about that market as it exists today, combined with what we can extrapolate from the three rapidly changing variables we've just described, it is possible to predict a dozen key factors—including speed, simplicity, limited brand loyalty, and continuous reinvention—in marketing and selling to such a fast-moving global audience:

SPEED

This is distinguished from the infrastructural speed (described above) that will be created by global wireless broadband. Here, we are talking about the need to proliferate the marketing/advertising message around the world, to all audiences, almost instantaneously. This means that the message, in all of its permutations dictated by language, culture, and politics, must be prepared in advance and delivered simultaneously. Otherwise you risk the bleeding over of one audience's customized message into that of another, potentially antagonistic audience . . . with potentially disastrous results. What this means—contrary to the flat-world view of the global marketplace—is that even if you manage to produce a product or service that fits everyone, no one marketing message in support of it will fit all.

SIMPLICITY

It has been noted over the last half-century, with considerable dismay, that the typical advertising campaign is targeted at an eighth-grade educational level . . . and falling. Well, get ready, because the next two billion consumers joining the global marketplace are likely to be far less educated than that—indeed, some sizable portion (20 percent? 50 percent?) will be functionally illiterate.

What this means is that for maximum customer reach, most companies will have to revamp their marketing message to perhaps the third-grade level—or even lower. This is going to necessarily limit the complexity of the message being conveyed, and will present an enormous challenge to marketers. Obviously, some companies may choose to create several messages, each aligned to a different level of audience education. But that will create its own challenges in identifying and reaching those different segments.

And that's only the beginning. There is also the matter of language itself. There are nearly seven thousand different living languages in the world today. Are companies willing to translate their message, even with more sophisticated automation tools than Babelfish, into all of those dialects? Most, one assumes, will choose to stick with the world's lingua franca, English (which will have its own long-term implications). But then, the question is, which English? British? American? Or that rapidly emerging international hybrid dialect "Globish"?

NONVERBAL

The most obvious solution to this problem of language and literacy is to simply limit the use of language to the spoken word and a very simple vocabulary—and then do all of the heavy lifting using nonverbal techniques: acting, iconography, graphics, animation, modeling, and so forth. As much as we admire commercials filled with clever and ironic dialog, the reality is that the future of global advertising may look a lot like a Mentos commercial: slapstick, highly visual, and almost wordless. College-educated viewers in China, the United States, and Europe may find them dumb, but they'll still watch—while the Next Two Billion will watch, understand, and buy.

LIMITED BRAND LOYALTY

Imagine now fifty million companies, all operating in the global marketplace, all clamoring for customer attention, all claiming to be better than their competitors, and all in a ferocious battle for dominance over a host of opponents around the world.

In this environment, no smart consumer would ever stick to a single brand over any extended period of time—certainly not unless one provider is so clearly superior to everyone else year after year that to buy from anyone else would be crazy. But in a global marketplace with even the narrowest market segment populated by scores of competitors, how often is that kind of enduring differentiation going to happen?

No, any competitive advantage is going to be quickly swarmed and copied. So any prudent consumer is simply going to ignore brands and go for the best deal in terms of price, performance, and image. The last will be driven by advertising, but the first two will most often come from the recommendations of trusted friends, peers, and acknowledged experts. And that in turn suggests the primary future task of public relations: to influence those opinion makers, as always, but directly and not through the increasingly obsolete traditional media.

(One caveat here: a countervailing force to all of this will be consumer laziness—that is, the exhaustion that comes from having to deal with too many selections, too much marketing noise, and too little time. This is likely to lead to a kind of ersatz product loyalty, which will confuse the seller into believing he or she has devoted customers—when in fact consumers just have not found sufficient motivation to switch. That motivation will ultimately come from the growing online army of reviewers, customer satisfaction surveys, and customer-profiling software.)

POWERFUL (BUT SIMPLE) BRAND RECOGNITION

This would seem to contradict the previous factor. But what we're talking about here is the iconography of great institutions, as opposed to their actual products and services. Certain images and names carry with them a powerful, almost totemic, resonance that will have a unique impact among the emerging new billions: Apple, Intel, KFC, Microsoft, Sony, Boeing, McDonald's, Oxford University, Coca-Cola, Toyota, Shell, and so on. These names and images carry a special weight and will always attract special attention—sometimes even after the company itself has lost its luster. Brand recognition doesn't guarantee that the consumer will automatically buy a company's offerings, but it will certainly garner those companies an extra look, and invest them with added respect. And since marketing to the new global marketplace will be all about capturing attention amidst the roar, even that brief moment of extra attention and respect may prove to be decisive.

CONTINUOUS REINVENTION

When you don't have brand loyalty beyond its crudest forms, then legacy becomes a much less important matter. The world doesn't much care about what you've done in the past—or even plan for the future—but only what you are offering right *now*. We've recently seen that the old notion of buying a Ford because you've always bought Fords is utterly obsolete. IBM abandoned its seventy-year-old computer business to become a service company, with barely a ripple in the marketplace.

But the single event that history will likely record as the turning point from the old marketplace to the new was Apple's decision to drop "Computer" from its official name in recognition of its giant leaps into first the consumer market with the iPod, then wireless with the iPhone. The implicit message was that it didn't matter what Apple was famous for, that its image was now infinitely malleable—that henceforth Apple would be free to become whatever company it wanted to be.

We can expect to see many more companies become chameleon-like in the years to come, especially as they realize that hanging on to the past not only confers no real advantages, but can be an unwise constraint. The good news in this is that companies that choose to compete in this new global market will be free to become whatever they want, and pursue whatever strategy they feel is most competitive and best serves their shareholders and employees. The bad news is that they are going to be much less able to depend upon sales to their existing customers as they move from one generation to the next.

DIGITAL DELIVERY (OR GLOBAL INFRASTRUCTURE)

The need for speed and simultaneity, combined with the lack of continuity among customers, argues that most companies that will play in the global marketplace will be driven toward the simplest, fastest, and most pervasive techniques for getting their products and services to customers. It goes without saying that the best way to do this is digitally and over the Internet. Not only is it faster than any nondigital delivery process, but thanks to Moore's Law, its advantages are only going to grow exponentially in the years to come.

For that reason, there will be a continuous pressure on companies to make their deliverables as virtual as possible—the less you have to physically move the better off you'll be. That means more and more one-time hardware platforms that are then upgraded online in firmware and software (e.g., Apple iTouch); local production for products designed using online tools (clothing, furniture, automobiles); ever richer and more interactive Web experiences (movies, games, television, and hybrids of the three); and teleconferencing and telepresence for many services (especially training and consulting).

Of course, it will be impossible to completely get away from some physical products. And that will be to the advantage of global delivery companies such as Federal Express and DHL. In fact, these companies—and those that take advantage of the new generation of short-hop jets to compete with them—are not only likely to find demand for their services skyrocketing as the Next Billions come onstream, but ironically to be given a further push as manufacturers and service providers reduce the physical presence of their deliverables from the kinds of things that require shipping containers and crates to items that can be stuffed into a FedEx envelope.

USER CONTROL

There is an even quicker way than the Internet to deliver products and services to millions of far-flung customers: let them perform their own design, manufacture, service, and support of your products. Design automation tools, robots, and computer-aided manufacturing, the continuous product miniaturization that is the by-product of Moore's Law, and perhaps someday nanotechnology will make it increasingly possible to move much of the design, manufacturing, and support cycles into the hands of the users themselves. Those users in turn, paradoxically, are likely to accept this added work and responsibility gladly because of the increased control—and improved likelihood of satisfaction with the finished product—that will result.

This is hardly a new idea. Over the last twenty years most small-scale publishing has moved from the print shop into the hands of users; photo processing is now done by individuals, as is much of the work of the postal service (e-mail and instant messaging). Meanwhile, a large fraction of the medical diagnostic work that used to be done only in hospitals has now moved, via ever smaller and smarter devices, into the doctor's office or even local "factories" (for example, laser eye surgery clinics). Millions of kids around the world now design their own T-shirts and construct their own virtual worlds (Second Life).

The necessity of getting sophisticated products, services, and experiences out to billions of people in comparatively remote parts of the world is going to force companies—even those whose deliverables are largely Web-based—to provide their customers with the tools to do their own creation. This will necessarily lead to some loss of control—but gaining power by surrendering control is the very heart of the twenty-first-century economy.

NEW FORMS OF FINANCING

The great lesson of the global economic crisis of 2008 was that our system of global credit and finance was not prepared to deal with the new realities of the twenty-first-century economy. Well, those challenges are only going to multiply as hundreds of millions of new consumers arrive in the global marketplace from societies built largely upon barter, with unreliable currencies, and few legal controls on fraud, bribery, and fraudulent contracts—and with many of these new consumers earning annual incomes of three digits.

These new consumers are going to need access to credit (and capital), not to mention considerable training in business ethics and etiquette, and a healthy legal (and global) enforcement apparatus. Those systems and agencies will emerge over time by necessity—because the alternative is economic chaos. And no doubt the interval between now and then is going to see even more global financial crises. That's the cost of growing up the world's economy—and the quicker these new institutions are in place, the less painful the transition will be.

But of immediate concern to businesses that will operate in this global marketplace is how to get enough buying power into the hands of these new consumers. The answer is credit. The good news is that the work of people such as Nobel laureate Muhammad Yunus of Grameen Bank in the area of microloans to the poor points to such a solution. Ironically, Yunus's technique involves enlisting groups of village women to dole out microloans and enforce payment among themselves—meaning that a large part of the global mass market will be driven by the other half of the world economy: millions of small microniche groups.

PRECISE CULTURAL AWARENESS

The twenty-first century has quickly disabused us of one of the great myths of the twentieth: that as we became increasingly interlinked via technology, travel, and commerce, mankind would become increasingly homogeneous—and that we would see the rise of a common global culture.

What we've discovered, often to our dismay, is that while two individuals on opposite sides of the planet may wear the same Levi's jeans and *Shrek* T-shirt, even listen to the same world music on their iPods and watch CNN, they may still hold utterly different concepts of the universe, of time and space, and of right and wrong. Indeed, they may both be plotting to kill the other, believing the other to be the embodiment of evil.

In other words, universal brotherhood doesn't seem to be coming any time soon.

What that means is that even as you are crafting your global promotion—keeping it simple, using largely nonverbal messaging—you are still going to have to be continually vigilant for any content that might be misread or perceived as a coded insult or slight by one culture or another around the world.

We are already seeing some of this. Take the tempest over the embossed lids of Burger King ice cream cones, which nearly led to a boycott in the United Kingdom after a Muslim customer saw in their design a slur against his faith: it may have seemed absurd, even risible to us in the West, but it nevertheless was very real to the people who saw themselves as victims. Obviously, some of these potential slights are so subtle that it will be almost impossible to detect beforehand. Nevertheless, the smart global company will have cultural critics and focus groups in place around the world just to make sure these faux pas don't do too much damage.

PRIVATE CURRENCY OR PERPETUAL ARBITRAGE

For companies operating in the global mass market, revenues are going to come from a wide array of financial instruments, from stable international credit cards down to volatile national currencies. Today, this mostly works because most of this exchange is based upon the largest global currencies, including the U.S. dollar and the euro.

But 2008 showed that in times of economic instability, even these monolithic currencies can become unpredictable, swinging wildly in their values and exchange rates. Imagine now hundreds of millions of new consumers attempting to pay in currencies like the Zimbabwe rand, which can change value by 1,000 percent in *one day*. In this scenario, it's possible to imagine a transaction becoming a net loss to the seller just in the time it takes to process the purchase.

What this suggests is that companies that operate in the global mass marketplace are going to have to become even more conscious of how they manage their money—to the point of actively conducting their own arbitrage and moving cash back and forth between currencies in real time in order to, if not make a further profit, then at least hold their own. The biggest companies will probably conduct this arbitrage in-house (as many already are), but we are also likely to see banking services arise just to handle this kind of work for the average global market player.

There is also a second, more extreme, scenario. As companies become even less rooted than they are today, as they arbitrage money back and forth between currencies in an attempt not to lose value, some may conclude that it would be far more efficient—and more profitable—to create their own currencies.

What would this "money" look like? We already have proven examples in use today: credits, frequent flier miles, coupons, et cetera. Will companies be willing to take the next step beyond these ersatz currencies and create real money that can be exchanged, invested, and would be subject to private Federal Reserve–like guarantees? Time will tell.

GEOGRAPHIC GYPSIES

We've just mentioned rootlessness, and this may become one of the defining characteristics of companies that choose to pursue the global mass market. Such firms will be so international in their outlook and (thanks to global interconnection) so physically scattered about the planet that the decision of where the company actually *is* will likely be less defined by history than opportunity. Companies will move to where they are most wanted by governments and customers.

What this means in practice is that this kind of company, at least, will become fungible. It will move its "headquarters," corporate registration, and tax identity as legally allowed to the most hospitable economic environment of the moment. To these companies, notions of national sovereignty are of little importance—look at the flight of global industry to business-friendly countries such as Dubai. And that should be a warning to individual nations: create an uncompetitive business environment and these companies, many of them among the largest in the world, will simply move on to somewhere else . . . and just about any attempt to tie them down will prove fruitless.

What Al-Qaeda Learned from Steve Jobs

Those are the factors at play for companies competing in the new global mass market. Obviously they present considerable challenges. But at the same time none of them are unprecedented—and, in fact, we have already begun to deal with most of them. Furthermore, as you look at these factors, certain marketing and sales strategies—some old, some new—present themselves.

Most obvious is the power of celebrity and name recognition. If you are trying to reach two or three billion people with your message, you are going to need to straddle barriers of income, education, language, and life experience . . . and the best way to do that is with a simple, accessible, and instantly recognizable message. The lesson of the last thirty years is that celebrity and fame may not close the sale, but they are almost unmatched at capturing attention and validating products and services. This suggests that the years to come are going to be a golden age for celebrity endorsements—but only for the biggest names in that category; an American television star, no matter how big, is less likely to capture the world's notice than even a mid-level Hollywood action hero or a Bollywood star.

Celebrity comes in many forms, of course, and one doesn't have to be an actor or actress to be famous (though it usually helps). For the last quarter of the twentieth century, it was said that Muhammad Ali was the best-known person on earth, though that title may now be usurped by Nelson Mandela, Osama bin Laden, Che Guevara, or Bill Clinton. In the business world, nobody equals the star power of Steve Jobs or Bill Gates, except perhaps Richard Branson. And, of course, there are the famous musicians, from Paul McCartney to the late Bob Marley.

Notice that this list does not distinguish between the revered and the infamous, or the living and the dead. The harsh reality is that in the new global mass market, fame has only magnitude, not valence—and if a mass murderer like Mao can be used to market handbags, so can bin Laden or some other terrorist. And this is going to raise some difficult ethical questions for many companies in developed countries that might not merit a second thought among the emerging companies of the developing world.

We titled this section "What Al-Qaeda Learned from Steve Jobs" only somewhat facetiously. In fact, the story of Apple following the return of cofounder Jobs in 1997 is paradigmatic of how to drive both a company and its leader into global fame and cultlike status. Jobs and Apple did this by wrapping a distinctive product with equally distinctive packaging and advertising—all of it cool and elegant, but also simple enough for even the least sophisticated audience to understand. This then was wrapped in the myth of Apple Computer itself, as embodied in the iconic candy-colored logo and image of "cool"—and carefully ignoring the company's catastrophic decade before Jobs's return. Finally, as the embodiment of Apple's maverick attitude, innovativeness, and cool, there was Jobs himself: enigmatic, with a checkered past, supremely confident and hip.

The total package was almost unbeatable. And when Apple began its run of landmark products—the iMac, the iPod, and the iPhone—the cult of Apple grew to include millions, with the company enjoying name recognition among billions of people, most of whom would never be able to afford any of the company's products.

This has been a lesson learned, if unconsciously (and usually incompletely), by many companies, groups, governments, and organizations. One of those, it seems obvious now, was Al-Qaeda. The composer Karlheinz Stockhausen took a lot of grief for his statement describing 9/11 as "the biggest work of art there has ever been," but in retrospect he was on to something. What were the attacks on the Pentagon and World Trade Center but global advertisements—simple to understand, unforgettable, nonverbal—for the arrival of an influential new group on the world scene? This, in turn, was wrapped in the image of Al-Qaeda itself: mysterious, ruthless, driven by religious fervor, obsessed with purity—and embodied in the enigmatic figure of Osama bin Laden himself, whose apparent survival has kept the world riveted on his next move for nearly a decade.

The fact that the reality of Al-Qaeda apparently has little to do with this image (Tora Bora proving to be just a dirty cave, not the high-tech lair of an Islamic Dr. No) is now almost immaterial: the image, especially among the multitudes of the developing world, is now set forever.

Memes, Bemes, and Gossip

Creating a cult of personality and a compelling corporate myth will be a powerful marketing tool for dealing with the emerging global mass market—especially for establishing that powerful brand recognition that will confer an enduring competitive advantage. But pulling it off, difficult in even the best environments, is going to become almost impossible in the cacophony of noise that will be coming off the new marketplace.

Most companies will likely respond with traditional advertising techniques, modified for the Internet age, and then supercharged (simple messages, high production values, new dissemination tools) to reach this expanded audience. But, as we've also learned in recent years, it is becoming very difficult for any advertisement or commercial message to rise above the roar and capture the audience's attention. Furthermore, audiences quickly develop a mental filter to screen out all but the most interesting ad messages—meaning that after a brief window of opportunity where they are still curious and receptive, most of those Next Billions will also begin tuning out ads.

But there is still one more way for companies to promote their wares to the mass global market—and this one, still in its earliest stages, may prove to be the most powerful of all.

Nothing moves faster—especially in the Internet age—than gossip, jokes, rumors, and urban myths. They proliferate so quickly that it sometimes seems that everyone in the wired world is getting the same story at the same time. Why is this process so pervasive and so quick? There seem to be two parts to the answer: (1) the story has some kind of entertainment value (shock, humor, fear, etc.); and (2) you feel compelled to share that story with others—and you have the technology at hand (e-mail, IM, online bulletin boards, Twitter) for doing so.

In other words, users voluntarily step up to become participants and distributors, sending the story along to multiple targets, who in turn do the same—resulting quickly in an exponential curve of dissemination,

So, the billion-dollar question for companies and other organizations becomes *Is there a way to replicate this process with our message?*

Yes, and we've already described it. As we noted in chapter 8, sociologists and linguists have a term for units of thought or language that are proliferated through a population: *memes.* Somewhat controversially, they even compare memes to pandemic viruses or to genes. We don't have to go that far to appreciate that when everyone we know around the world, seemingly unprompted, is watching the same viral video *at the same time,* something extraordinary is going on.

We also know that sometimes these memes can be intentionally created with a distinct purpose and proliferated. In recent years we have seen company stock prices crash based upon flash rumors that appeared out of nowhere, yet appear to have been invented specifically to be destructive (such as the rumor of Steve Jobs having a heart attack). Billions of dollars of net worth have swung back and forth between the time one of these rumors hit and the moment when the nation, company, or individual successfully managed to disavow it. In the very first days of 2009, as Israel attacked Hamas in Gaza, supporters of both sides flooded the Web with videos (many of them fake), photographs (ditto), Web site comments, and blogs, all trying to hijack the global dialog on the events as they unfolded.

All of this suggests that it may well be possible to consciously construct and proliferate "directed" memes. And if that is the case, then there is no obvious reason why a business might not make part of, or even the heart of, its marketing operation the creation of such memes.

As we've already read, Tom has labeled these "directed," mutually rewarding memes *bemes*. And as any reporter will tell you, bemes are not without precedent. The media and the business world have long had a secret relationship in which certain ambitious executives will intentionally "leak" stories on upcoming products, management changes, layoffs, internal feuds, and so on. They have done this in hopes of disseminating these stories—and lining up customers, attacking competitors, taking personal credit—all without leaving any of their own fingerprints on the message. Some very successful business leaders, some of whom you might not suspect of such chicanery, are quite good at this kind of controlled leakage—and have used it to their considerable advantage.

In this light, bemes would seem to be the natural evolution of this technique onto the global stage. Now, the traditional media would be used a lot less, and the blogosphere, chat rooms, friends lists on social networks, contacts on LinkedIn, and the like would be used a lot more. In the fast-moving world of the global mass market, nothing could be more powerful than a company marketing message that, sub rosa, reaches billions of people at almost the same moment, drives a burst of several million new orders, then disappears without a trace.

For companies, this may all sound good, but there's one problem: right now, there is no science of bemes. In fact, there is no standardized body of techniques for successfully creating them. Most of the successful or destructive examples we know about appear to have been one-offs, the product of serendipity and luck more than anything else.

But the potential power of bemes is so great that it is hard to imagine that there won't be a discipline that arises around it, that successful techniques won't be shared, and that the use of bemes and other forms of self-replicating, self-proliferating marketing and promotion won't soon become a major part of selling to the global market.

The Mass Local Market

Now, let's look at the other side of the modern economy: the millions of small groups and microniche markets that will emerge in parallel to the creation of the global mass market. Let's call the art (and it will be an art as much as a science) of selling to these groups *mass handselling.*

As you'll see, this other world is almost the exact opposite of the global mass market—which stands to reason when you consider that each will largely exist in *response* to the apparent weaknesses of the other.

Like the global mass market, the mass niche market will feature its own giant forces, key factors, and distinctive marketing tools.

This time, the giant forces include membership, culture, content quality, and duration of the message:

Membership—Membership is *the* sine qua non of the mass niche world. It is the response to the anomie of the mass global market, the source of meaning in one's social relationships in the twenty-first century, and it provides self-definition in an increasingly anonymous wired culture. We will be joining groups because we want membership in associations that matter, that endure, and that give us purpose. In exchange, membership in those groups will offer us security, a common language and culture, and a web of deep relationships. Any company that wants to market to one of these groups is not only going to have to understand this dynamic, but also to obtain some kind of "membership" of its own in that group in order to be trusted enough to offer its wares.

Culture—All associations, if they exist over time and are sufficiently insular, will develop a culture of their own,

complete with a private etiquette, mores, jargon, rules, rewards and punishments, initiations and honors, and barriers to entry by outsiders. Depending upon their purpose
and duration (see below) nearly every group will develop
its own culture. Some will be rudimentary and simple,
others (especially in groups that last generations) as subtle and complex as anything found in human history.

Quality of content—Culture is only half of the story, the
glue that binds groups and holds them together. But what
keeps groups dynamic, productive, and attractive to their
members ultimately comes down to what they offer members in regards to their organizing theme. If you are part
of a group interested in, say, Shaker boxes or weather-
related applications for the Google Android phone or
environmental causes of childhood autism, then those
groups had better provide you with an experience—
news, conversation, expertise, emotional support, technical assistance, resource libraries, product discounts—that
makes the time you spend there worth the effort.

Duration—If speed is the clock of the global mass market, *duration* is its counterpart in the mass niche market.
Groups exist to provide continuity for their members, but
the appeal of a group only lasts as long as it is useful. For
that reason, no matter how strong the "glue" of culture,
a group that loses its purpose will soon disintegrate. Thus
it's likely that the millions of groups that will emerge in
the new economic order will exhibit life spans that range
literally from minutes to a century or more. And as we'll
soon see, that creates some singular challenges for companies trying to sell to them.

As you may have already noted, these dominant forces driving the mass niche market are much more complex, irrational,

and thus ultimately more *powerful* (because they touch deeper instincts) than their equally irrational, but less complicated, counterparts in the global mass market. You'll *want* the stuff available on the mass market, but you'll *need* the experiences delivered by the niches.

This fact will likely (and perversely) make the mass niche world, despite its surface calm and apparent stability, even more volatile and emotional—and in some ways less predictable—than the more obviously chaotic global mass market.

Marketing to a Million Niches

Now, let's look at the key factors defining how to market and sell to the mass niche market. Once again, they are largely the obverse of those we saw as defining the global mass market.

Key factors:

Membership—This is the smaller version of the large force described above. In this case, "membership" describes the need of each individual group to locate, recruit, and maintain members. This is going to be an ongoing, relentless, and unforgiving challenge to all but the most stable groups—and they will need a wide range of tools and techniques, including specialized search, presentational tools, record-keeping, and file management. Because no two groups will be alike, either in culture or duration, all of these products and services will themselves have to be customized either by the seller or the group itself.

Mass customization—Customizing products and services—design, content, delivery, and support—is going to be a part of every transaction in the new economy, whether it is for the mass market or mass niches. However, it is likely to be much more sophisticated (and usually more expensive) when applied to the mass niche world. That's because, unlike the mass global market, where customization will be mostly used as a safeguard against cultural errors and to reduce the cost of delivery, in the world of mass niches customization will be a necessary requirement to make the product or service precisely congruent with the needs and cultures of each individual niche—because otherwise they will be denied entry. And, as much as these niches will prefer to do the customizing themselves, most will be unable to do so.

> *Mass handselling means companies that want to operate in this marketplace are going to have to do much of the customizing themselves. This will be more expensive, but groups will be willing to pay more for what they need. And smart groups will quickly learn to set their unique requirements "on the front porch," so to speak—that is, on the public part of their Web sites—for tradesmen passing by to inspect and modify their deliverables.*
>
> *Companies, meanwhile, will increasingly make use of "spiders" and other Web information gathering tools to seek out and gather up this information and, when possible, use it to modify their offerings. Those companies that do this the most efficiently and effectively will find themselves increasingly welcome into groups—and thus begin to enjoy the benefits of a long-term business relationship.*

Richness of message—Microniche groups are all about quality of experience, and that will be the field that they compete on with their competitors. Habit and comfort will only hold members for a while; should another group offer a superior experience, there will be few technical barriers to switching. For that reason, most groups are going to be hungry for anything that enables them to improve the quality of their content—and that is likely to include better hardware (servers, displays, cameras), software (groupware, teleconferencing, editing suites), content management, and business/accounting software.

In some sectors, especially ones where membership is rewarded with wealth, influence, or social power, it wouldn't be surprising to see technological "arms races" develop, as groups vie for a reputation for the best experience in order to capture the highest-quality members. Companies that position themselves as enablers to competition are likely to be in much demand.

Conversation—After all of the services, databases, and connections, the value of groups will ultimately come down to conversation. As we've already noted, aiding and improving the quality of this conversation will be a major market for companies of all kinds. But there is a second factor here as well: to successfully market and sell to these groups, a provider must be prepared to join the conversation. If selling to the mass global market is all about simple, mostly nonverbal messaging, then selling to the mass niche market is about complex, largely verbal messages spoken in the lingua franca of that group.

This doesn't mean pure fluency in every private language of a million microniche groups, no more than doing business around the world today means speaking every single local native dialect. But it does mean speaking to individual groups in a manner that shows some degree of research and diligence into the dominant symbols and phrases of those groups. Happily, most of that knowledge can be gathered automatically from the Web—and then further nuanced over time (also automatically) through interactions with those groups.

Powerful brand loyalty—This, one might say, is the payoff. Unlike in the global mass market, among microniche groups dedication will pay off handsomely in terms of long-term loyalty. It will be so difficult to get inside these groups that, once in, as with citizens of a small town, it will be difficult to do anything so bad that you are exiled. Indeed, most groups will accept a fair amount of increased price, reduced quality, or lack of timeliness from a vendor who has been accepted inside their walls.

As we'll note later in the book, this kind of loyalty can make a vendor lazy and it enforces a lack of innovation that ultimately could be dangerous, but those are the kinds of problems most companies would love to have—especially as a by-product of a stable and predictable customer base that might stay intact for decades.

Powerful brand recognition (complex)—In the global mass market, what brand recognition that will survive will be mostly simple: Apple = Cool, Tiffany's = Expensive, Toyota = Reliable, Pixar = Entertaining. But in the world of microniche groups, just the opposite will be true. The vetting process to allow a vendor into a group will be so long and complicated—word of mouth, committees, field testing, even interviews—that these customers are likely to know almost as much about the company as most of its employees do.

The good news in this is that groups are likely to be excellent customers: knowledgeable, patient, with extremely useful input on future directions for the company, and willingly to consider expanding the relationship to include other product lines and services. The bad news is they will also be particularly demanding, especially when they realize what control they have over the fate of their "family" companies.

Durability—As already noted, these groups have the potential to be as evanescent or enduring as any collection of human beings. And what is needed to effectively serve, say, a group of software engineers in Lithuania brought together on a contract to create a dozen lines of valuable code for a client, is very different from what is required to meet the needs of a local historical society in Kansas that has been together for three generations.

Not only will it be necessary to adapt your message to the special interests of hundreds, even thousands of these groups, now you must also put into your marketing equation the expected life span of the group as well.

On the one hand, with your group of code writers, you may have only minutes to deliver your message (ironically, they are a more evanescent market than anything a global mass marketer will ever face); while with the Kansas historical society you might have a century. Perhaps the best way to describe the challenge is to call it fourth-dimensional marketing, or perhaps Marketing 4.0.

If Marketing 1.0 is traditional real-world marketing, 2.0 is marketing to the Web, and 3.0 is the world of bemes and social networks, Marketing 4.0 might be simply described as Marketing 3.0 under the constraints of relative time. Not only do you have to use the latest marketing techniques, operate on multiple platforms from laptops to mobile phones to embedded systems, mass-customize the message to numerous small groups (all while earning their trust), but also you have to do it all successfully under the regime of an equal number of clocks.

The mere thought of all this can be pretty dispiriting— and enough to make all but the most ambitious companies consider taking their chances out in the Wild West of the global marketplace. But don't forget: there will be some extraordinary advantages to this kind of selling as well.

For example, whatever support that code-writing team needs it's going to want right now. The duration of the decision curve will be essentially zero. No guarantees, no warranties, no service, and probably no support. It will be basing its decision largely on what its members already know—that is, on a company's reputation. If you have that recognition and image, you could find yourself in the enviable position of selling to ten thousand of these "InstanTeams" per day.

Conversely, once you find a way to sell your product or service to one of those "PermanenTeams," like our Kansas historical society, you might find yourself with a steady source of business that will one day be serviced by your grandchildren. What company wouldn't like to have that kind of stability in at least one part of its operations? Imagine your credit rating when some percentage of your customer base is all but guaranteed for revenues into the next century.

This, in turn, raises another interesting point. We keep talking about how difficult it will be to market to all of these bubbles, about the need to approach them from the bottom up and inside out, rather than the traditional top down and outside in. Yet it is probably a mistake to assume that this different approach will be necessary for more than a fraction—let's say half—of all of those emerging microniches.

Why? Well, consider our team of programmers. Whatever they need, they need right now—and they are going to be out hunting for it without too much concern for trust or even reliability. The trick to marketing to them is to be in their path when they head out on the hunt, and that probably means using some of those established tricks of brand marketing (supercharged, of course, for the new global market) over the new channels created by social networks, broadband wireless, and mobile. And, of course, building a reputation for quality.

Conversely, think about that century-long customer. Sure, it will take a long time to earn the trust of that microniche. But then, you've got a long time. Is a couple years' work worth a century of business? You bet it is.

User-enlisted design, manufacture, and service—As we've already pointed out, many groups, because of their deep knowledge of your business, will be extremely useful in helping you design products and services uniquely suited to meet their needs. However, and this is distinct from the global mass market, niche group members are not going to be particularly interested in helping you create those products. As most people will spend their days inhabiting both marketplaces, they will already be doing a lot of self-configuring, self-manufacturing, and self-servicing—and one of the underlying reasons for joining groups is to get away from these kinds of demands. So, although groups will be hugely helpful in conceptualizing future products and services, they will be little help in the execution of those designs.

Private banking—We mentioned in the section on the global mass market that some companies may choose to create their own system of credit, currency, and exchange rates in order to escape the volatility of the world financial markets. By comparison, groups, because of their deep interconnectedness and mutual trust, may gravitate toward pooling and managing their own money. This is hardly unprecedented: shtetl Jews, Vietnamese, and Hmong immigrants to America, certain caste Hindus, and hundreds of other ethnic groups have long developed their own private banking and investment networks outside the traditional financial industry. Grameen Bank, with its microloans, is simply a cultural variant of this, operating within small villages. All offer superior terms for loans because they can reduce risk by exerting severe social penalties on those who default. Tight, enduring groups like those we will see emerging in the years to come are perfect candidates for this type of arrangement— and smart financial institutions, instead of trying to stop them, will provide the tools and the security systems to empower them.

Precise community awareness—We reminded ourselves in the global mass market section that the world isn't flat after all, and that companies operating on the global stage still have to be ever vigilant not to unconsciously violate any local taboos, misuse loaded terms, or cross local cultural laws. With microniche groups the same is true, only this time the danger lies within the tiny communities themselves. Each will have its own rules, and its own taboos—and while an outside vendor will be excused for the occasional slip, there are certain boundaries they cannot cross without being exiled forever.

> *Obviously, there is no easy way to determine what these taboos are, so once again the best solution is vigilance. You need to move slowly at first, keeping track of mistakes so they aren't repeated, and building the relationship over time to build trust.*

Private exchange—We've already mentioned private banking and finance within groups, but there is also the likelihood of groups creating their own microeconomies—buying whenever possible from one another's businesses (the considerable precedent of a local Chamber of Commerce or service organization), hiring one another for outside work, even noncash exchange systems such as barter. The vendor who has worked for many years with a group may find itself, as a sign of their commitment, asked to participate in these private exchanges—and had better be prepared to do so.

Iconic image—If rootlessness and a protean style characterize companies selling to the global mass market, rootedness and a sense of permanence are vital to the image of a company serving the mass niche audience. That doesn't mean that the latter can't be protean companies—on the contrary, they will probably have to be to deal with all of this divergent demand—but they can't seem to be shapeshifters. What groups want are vendors who don't change, who are endlessly reliable, and about whom they rarely have to think.

> *What this suggests is that companies dealing with the mass market will sell their "cloud" of ever-changing operations, their mutability; while companies dealing with groups will sell their "cores," the unchanging, predictable corporate centers.*

Family Style

The single most important marketing tool for companies handselling to the millions of microniche groups that will emerge in the years to come is *trust*, in all of the forms that trust will take. We'll get into this more in the final section of the book, but for now the key point is that trust is the currency of the mass niche marketplace.

Companies may still use gossip, bemes, and mass advertising as a backdoor way to raise brand awareness, capturing the attention of group members when they are out in the world in their mass market mode. But when it comes down to closing the deal and building a long-term relationship with a group, it will all come down to trust. Groups will vet potential new vendors by looking to trusted sources for advice—the experiences of their members, existing customers, reviewers, bloggers, and the trade press.

Once they become customers, they will look to other forms of trust: reliability, responsiveness, security, privacy, and openness. They will be forgiving, but they will never forget—and so a vendor that has years of apparently happy relationship with a group may suddenly find itself locked out with little warning, having crossed an unwritten line where its failures of trust can no longer be forgiven. If this sounds like the dynamics of family life, it's because it is.

This will be a tough standard to maintain, but any company that attempts it will undoubtedly be a better organization for the effort and discipline required. And it will enjoy a financial stability that is rare in these crazy times.

PART FOUR

LOVE MONEY

The World After Material

CHAPTER 10

NEW SYSTEMS OF TRUST

Adding Context to Commerce

> For it is mutual trust, even more than mutual interest
> that holds human associations together.
> —H. L. MENCKEN

We've now spent nine chapters on the mechanisms and processes of the transformed, fragmented global economy that is being created by the Web and the technology revolution behind it.

Though we have not been explicit about the fact, it should be obvious to the reader that the two dominant forces driving the new economy are money and human relationships—social capital. In one respect, this has always been true—yet the balance between the two has swung wildly over the last decade.

Before the turn of the twenty-first century, the business of business was largely business—that is, the sole empirical measure of a company's health and relative success was its balance sheet. More subjective factors—such as employee morale, customer happiness and loyalty, influence on competitors, cultural impact, brand identification—were relegated, if valued at all, to that catchall entry on the balance sheet: *goodwill*.

But a funny thing happened beginning in the late 1990s.

With the rise of one generation after another of new high-tech companies—software developers, online retailers, dot-coms, social networks—the traditional tools of accounting became increasingly incapable of capturing the real value of the business entities they were designed to describe. And that "goodwill" entry, once a patchwork tool to match the book value of a company to its actual sale price, suddenly began to take on more and more value—until, with the rise of the Web 1.0 world of companies such as eBay, Amazon, and Yahoo!, the value of "goodwill" (now increasingly described as "intangible assets" or "intellectual capital") often exceeded the company's official "book value."

Something was clearly amiss in the way we evaluated corporate worth. We were flying blind—which usually means we're headed for disaster. It came in early 2000, when the dot-com bubble, worth an estimated $1 trillion, burst, killing off several thousand new companies and putting hundreds of thousands of workers on the unemployment line. What is apparent now is not just that the values of these companies were vastly inflated by investor hysteria, but that the hysteria itself was largely driven by the lack of an accurate measurement system to assess true value. The result was hundreds of young companies, employing just a few dozen inexperienced entrepreneurs, competing against dozens of similar competitors over markets of unknown size and no obvious profitability—with some of these companies being valued in the billions by the stock market.

It's easy to look back now in amusement and disbelief at the stupidity of investors during the dot-com bubble. But let's not forget that there were a number of companies, including those listed above, that not only survived the crash, but more important, *ultimately lived up to their overwrought valuations during the boom.*

No company exemplifies this better than Amazon.com. One of the biggest survivors of the dot-com crash, Amazon continued to grow at an explosive rate until it ultimately dominated book sales in the United States and most of the rest of the world. Its market share, revenues, and stock price kept pace—despite the fact that the company seemed inherently unable to ever turn a profit. Then, almost a decade after its founding, and long after both the media and analysts had turned Amazon's endless red ink into something of a joke, the company suddenly turned profitable. It hasn't looked back.

The same can be said for a much different corporation, Apple, the most famous company of our time. Apple Computer, as it was then called, had already enjoyed its time in the spotlight, from the introduction of the Apple I in 1976 to the announcement of the Macintosh in 1984. Since then, especially after the departure of Steve Jobs, Apple had slowly slid into a genteel middle age, its onetime near-monopoly on personal computers slumping to a single-digit market share. By the mid-1990s it was generally assumed that Apple Computer was doomed to become a mere niche player, selling primarily to graphic artists and designers.

The story of Jobs's return to Apple and the company's extraordinary turnaround is well known. But the crucial point for our purposes is that it wasn't long before Apple's stock, and thus the company's value, outpaced the company's actual performance. In essence, the world had come to believe that Jobs would lead Apple to new heights of success, and would produce one innovative new technology after another, long before the company actually did introduce the iPod, iPhone, et cetera—and even longer before the benefits of those innovations began to show up on the company's balance sheet.

Last, but certainly not least, there is Google—perhaps the

most remarkable twenty-first-century business story to date. Its stock has been one of the greatest high-fliers of all time, and enduring enough to defeat any claims of market hysteria. At the same time, the company's total market valuation—at times greater than the entire automotive industry—is only remotely related either to Google's revenues or to its profits. On the other hand, what it does correlate to is Google's share of the Internet search market, where the company utterly dominates. Investors seem to hold to the belief that *if you have the right business model and a critical mass of users, the money will inevitably follow.*

It is a dictum that has become a kind of unwritten law for the Web 2.0 world. There, companies can race to millions of members (in the case of Facebook and MySpace, tens of millions) without a well-defined revenue model. Indeed, one of the most celebrated companies of this new world, Twitter, announced that it didn't even intend to address revenues until its third year of business. Yet investors (including veteran venture capitalists) have given these companies huge valuations: for example, YouTube, which had almost no revenues, was still sold to Google for a total of $8 *billion.* LinkedIn, the professional networking community, has an estimated $100 million in sales, and a $1 billion valuation. And the list goes on.

In fact, so attenuated has this revenue/profit date become that industry observers now talk of "Web 3.0," which is the impending era when Web 2.0 companies actually begin to make real money.

There have always been companies—IBM in the 1960s, Hewlett-Packard in the 1970s, Wal-Mart in the 1980s—that, through superior quality, innovation, service, influence, or just sheer industry dominance, are perceived by both customers and the overall marketplace as more valuable than they appear on paper. But historically, these have always been singular and ex-

traordinary companies; only now, for the first time, are we seeing entire *categories* of firms exhibiting these traits.

We could embark on a long digression into why traditional
accounting methods have failed (and why nothing has taken their
place), but that is for another time. What is important to recognize now is that, in one industry after another, companies are
being valued for a whole host of "other" assets that don't appear
on the balance sheet.

But it isn't enough to stop there. We must also ask: is there
some deep force that underpins these intangible assets?

In fact there is, and ironically we can find a clue in the old-
fashioned accounting term for this added value. What, after all,
is *goodwill*? It is Reputation, certainly; a long-standing pattern
of behavior that is in some way superior to the common run.
But reputation only looks backward. What is also needed is
Trust, the belief, based upon past interactions, that the company
will continue to maintain its reputation, that it will continue
to be, to some degree, extraordinary, and that it will not betray
the expectations of its employees, customers, partners, and investors.

Trust is our hidden factor. And, as the rise of entire industries
of low value/high valuation companies suggests, we have entered
into an era where Trust will become paramount.

But Trust, as we shall soon see, is not a monolithic concept.
It not only comes in several forms, but even changes with both
the context and (surprisingly) the location.

This first form of Trust, the underlying engine of corporate
goodwill and oversized valuations, the intuitive appreciation that
each of us has for the intangible assets of a company that do not
appear on the balance sheet, we'll call *Institutional Trust*. But as
pervasive as it has become, it is not alone, nor will it dominate
the emerging Web-based, fragmented global market to come. Ultimately, others will prove even more dominant.

A New World of Trust

It isn't just on the balance sheet and the stock ticker that Trust is in ascendance.

In 1999, the global public relations firm Edelman embarked on an international project to survey the commonalities and differences in Trust in nations around the world. By 2007, the survey had not only become an internationally recognized measure of what Edelman itself called "A Changing World Order of Trust," but over the course of the intervening eight years had reached some profound conclusions about the variations in the way people trust one another and institutions around the world.

The survey itself has become a sophisticated operation, every year conducting half-hour interviews each with 3,100 "opinion elites" (college-educated, age thirty-five to sixty-four, upper quartile income) located in eighteen nations—the United States, China, the United Kingdom, Germany, France, Italy, Spain, the Netherlands, Sweden, Poland, Russia, Ireland, Mexico, Brazil, Canada, Japan, South Korea, and India . . . in other words, the people most likely to pioneer the new Web-based global economy and set the pattern for the next two billion (including the poor in their own countries) who will follow.

Edelman's 2007 conclusions?

Trust Is a Market Asset
The current market is very fluid.

The old order is changing—showing signs of "global schisms, economic disparity, and an erosion of trust in traditional icons."

One of the most remarkable schisms that the Edelman survey discovered was the divergence in trust for cultural institutions between developed and developing nations. In particular, the survey found that developing countries "put more trust in business, brands, CEOs and sources of information than do mature, developed countries." By comparison, in developed countries studied, Edelman found that trust in business was much lower (47 percent compared to 60 percent), with the new embodiment of trustworthiness becoming nongovernmental organizations (NGOs) such as foundations, nonprofits, environmental groups, international aid agencies, and the like.

Interestingly, everywhere in the world, developed or developing nations, governments had the lowest trust ratings behind business, media, NGOs, and religion—except in Asia.

The deeper you dig into these results, the more interesting they become. For example, though the relative rankings of these five cultural institutions remain generally fixed for each of these countries, they nevertheless show a lot of variation over time— and occasionally switch position with their nearest neighbor on the list. Another interesting fact: with the exception of the Russians, companies based in developed nations are universally more trusted than those that are not. By the same token, though it is generally *assumed* around the world that businesses are a net good for society, Brits and Germans do not share that view, instead placing their trust in NGOs.

Meanwhile, in most of the world—especially the Americas— the person you are most likely to trust is most like yourself. But that isn't true in France and Russia, where less than a third of the respondents felt that way—the former apparently placing greater trust in experts, the latter on outsiders and foreigners. But the definition of that "person like me" also varies— "common interests" is a universal criterion, but "gender" and "nationality" trust varies between the developed and developing world.

We list these findings not to render a judgment on one society over another, but to make a point: who and what we trust, and the very nature of that trust itself, varies by region, by nation, and, we suspect—had the Edelman survey been of even finer granularity—by communities, perhaps even neighborhoods. Moreover, these results have been elicited from some of the most worldly—the most globalized—citizens of these nations. One can assume that all of these differences are only amplified in the general populations.

Let's call this factor *Cultural Trust*—and for now, the message is that when it comes to earning trust around the world, there is no one-size-fits-all solution. Rather, Trust earning methods must be "mass-customized"—that is, customized on an unprecedentedly vast scale—by institutions.

Edelman isn't the first to recognize the variable nature of Cultural Trust around the world. In 1995, after *The End of History*, Francis Fukuyama wrote a second book that was much less influential—but may prove more accurate—than its predecessor.

The book was entitled *Trust*, and subtitled *The Social Virtues and the Creation of Prosperity*. Fukuyama's thesis? To quote one sociology review: ". . . the culture of trust is the source of spontaneous sociability that allows enterprises to grow beyond family into professionally managed organizations."

What this means is that when you look around the world at different societies and their economies, it quickly becomes apparent that if you hold all other variables as comparatively equal, there still remains some "X Factor" that makes certain societies more successful than others.

For Fukuyama this X Factor is the greater ability of some societies than others to build large-scale corporations. And what underlies this ability? *Trust,* Fukuyama says, as made manifest by each nation's ability to move beyond kinship-based organizations (mostly small businesses) to larger and more complex "voluntary associations" (such as publicly traded corporations).

"One of the most important lessons we can learn from the examination of economic life is that a nation's well-being, as well as its ability to compete, is conditioned by a single, pervasive cultural characteristic: the level of trust inherent in the society."

Among the nations that Fukuyama places in the "low non-kinship trust" category are China, South Korea, Italy, and France. Among high-trust societies, he lists Japan, Germany, and the United States.

The criteria Fukuyama uses to make these categorizations are too complex to go into in much detail here, but ultimately it comes down to two factors: a society's beliefs and its values. For example, Fukuyama points to China, where a combination of Confucianism (with its deep stress upon family) and rules of inheritance (estates are divided among all male members) enables that nation to create millions of small companies, but impedes its ability to construct large ones.

From the calculus of these factors, Fukuyama believes, comes the level of trust a society exhibits, and ultimately, how well that society can create large corporations and compete in the emerging global economy. He also believes that these beliefs and values endure because they are "inherited ethical habits"; they are part of the cultural patrimony of a given society, and thus almost invisible to those within it.

In particular, Fukuyama holds that societies set a kind of unwritten limit on how much "social capital"— which in his definition means "the ability of people to work together for common purposes in groups and organizations"—its citizens can earn. Thus, for example, in low-trust societies, almost all so-cial capital derives from "familial" associations, with little credit (even a stigma) attached to dealing with "outsiders." High-trust nations, by comparison, while still retaining much of the social capital attached to family, also extend it outward to embrace "voluntary associations"—clubs, fraternal groups, societies—that by definition include non-kin associates, even strangers.

Fukuyama bolsters his argument by looking at enclaves of low trust within larger high-trust societies, such as African Americans in the United States and the schism between north-ern and southern Italy. For the former, he argues, the long era of slavery in black American history inculcated an understandable distrust of strangers and institutions that has limited that minor-ity economically. By the same token, southern Italy, populated by poor farmers who were driven off their land, developed a culture of not trusting anyone who was not kin—and that has prevented it from creating the big commercial enterprises found in the country's high-trust North.

By comparison, Japan, which is typically seen as an insu-lar, communitarian society, does in fact exhibit high levels of trust, Fukuyama says, because its culture demands that citizens participate in the community (and nation) beyond the family.

As one might imagine, Fukuyama's views on Trust were met with skepticism almost from the moment the book appeared. The biggest criticism had to do with his choices for low-trust and high-trust societies: they didn't seem congruent with Fuku-yama's own predictions for which of those societies would be able to create large corporations and thus be successful in the global economy. After all, weren't France and Italy wealthy na-tions with large companies? As one of the Four Tigers, wasn't Korea enjoying historic growth and prosperity? And, of course, there was China, enjoying economic growth that was the envy of the world. How could these nations possibly be categorized as uncompetitive?

Fukuyama's explanation was that corporate capitalism wasn't the only strategy to compete on the world stage, but that it was likely over time to be the best one. There were, in fact, a number of policies that low-trust societies could adopt that would allow them to circumvent their inherent limitations, the most notable being through government intervention and support. This, he said, is particularly true in France, where the family is central, and the one large organization to which the best and brightest aspire is the federal bureaucracy. The same is true in Korea, where the government actively supports the creation of large multinational corporations.

The biggest problem with this governmental strategy, says Fukuyama, is that it tends to hollow out the economy, creating a society with a few giant companies, a vast body of small family companies—and few midsized companies in between.

Another strategy for low-trust societies to succeed on the world stage, though Fukuyama doesn't explicitly say it, is through technology. In an interconnected world, it is possible for small companies—if they are smart—to successfully compete globally. From the single family group of artisans selling items from Africa to the world via eBay, to teams of Indian Institute of Technology engineering graduates in Bangalore selling their services online to distant contractors, to European clothing designers opening their fashion shows to the world through streaming video, technology can be the glue that local culture cannot provide.

China can be said to epitomize this approach. Though most of the attention goes to the large, government- (and usually Party-) backed enterprises, most of the real economic power in

China comes from where it always has: hundreds of thousands of small family-owned businesses that are increasingly skillful at marketing and selling their goods internationally.

Trusting Our Machines

A third, and very new, form of Trust has entered into our lives almost without being noticed. We'll call this *Technological Trust*. And for the little that most of us have noticed it, this technological trust has already had a profound impact on our lives.

Technological Trust is the process by which we first encounter a new technology, slowly adopt it, and then allow it into our lives so completely that not only can we hardly remember how we lived without it, but we hardly even realize we are using it. The personal computer, cable television, the cell phone, word processing, e-mail, the Internet, search engines, video players, digital displays, computer mice . . . the list now includes hundreds of items.

History suggests that this complete cycle from first encounter to total assimilation into the culture can take a couple years for a new product technology (for example, the iPod and other MP3 players) to a full human generation of about twenty years for a technological revolution (for example, the Internet, which took almost thirty years from invention to full cultural acceptance).

Technological trust plays an important role in this process. Actually learning how to use a new technology, especially a consumer product—even to becoming proficient—rarely takes more than a few weeks or months. But *trusting* that new technology to assume some long-established activity in one's life (writing letters, making phone calls, going to the library, shopping at the store) is a much longer process. And rightly so. This learning curve is slightly abbreviated among the growing number of people who have adopted dozens of these new technologies over the course of their lives, but it never completely disappears.

What interests us in this discussion is not what happens before a technology is adopted, but *after*, when acceptance becomes assimilation and what was novel becomes the quotidian. That is, what happens beyond that moment when we finally embrace the new technology as our own, and award it our trust.

When that happens, something remarkable takes place, particularly when that technology is in some way connected (as most are these days) to the Internet: then our trust not only encompasses the technology itself, but extends around the world. Open an e-mail account and soon enough you find yourself accustomed to receiving hundreds of "letters" each month from people you don't know, and who are located all over the globe: old friends who found your e-mail address in a Google search; spammers, digital newsletters, jokes, retailers you've recently purchased from, Nigerian 419 scam artists, and on and on. Even the worst excesses of traditional junk mail never came close to this.

Similarly, take the experience of searching the Web. To do so, you typically need a personal computer or some other intelligent device with an operating system, a modem, Internet access, and a search engine site.

Tellingly, the *instant* you turn on your computer and plug in the modem, you are already sharing private information with your Internet service provider—a company you likely know little about. Boot up your operating system and, if a bug is found, your computer sends a message to the manufacturer.

But your de facto acceptance of trust in strangers in cyberspace really explodes the instant you decide to search the Web. From the very first Web page you visit, your online travels are being tracked. Conduct a Google search and that company tracks your query—though it promises (and you trust) that it will not identify you and will erase that record after a few months. Software "cookies" and spyware programs are added to your computer just about every place you visit—unless you use antispyware software, which itself tracks your passage.

But the real fun starts when you make a transaction— especially when you use your credit card—on the Web. You can be certain not only that your purchase has been tracked and recorded, along with any information that can be gleaned from your credit card, but thanks to powerful behavioral software in place at sites like Amazon, that your current purchase will enter into a database of previous purchases that will be used to predict what you are likely to purchase next—and reconfigure the entire site to present the most appealing message to you.

This trust in the *processes* of technology is only part of the story. An even more interesting phenomenon is our growing— and some would say, inexplicable—trust in the *culture* of technology.

For example, most of us have had the experience of buying something on the Web and never even checking where the seller is located. And even if we do notice the location, we know nothing about the nature of the seller itself beyond, at best, some anecdotal comments from previous customers. In the real world, imagine getting on the phone and calling a retailer whose area code you don't recognize, whose office could be anything from a skyscraper to the trunk of a stolen car, who only shows you a photograph of the item he claims to have in inventory, and who gives you a list of happy past customers whose names you don't know, whom you have never met, and who would be almost impossible to contact.

Few of us would ever accept that arrangement in real life, yet millions of us do it every day on eBay. Even more remarkably, we aren't just talking about making such a transaction in our own culture, but in other countries that we know little about, that may have entirely different attitudes and laws about copyright and fraud, and—as we've just seen—may operate on entirely different rules of trust.

Yet we continue to do so, even in the face of global Internet viruses, con artists, and rip-offs—experiences that, were they to occur to us at a shopping mall, would probably drive us away from the venue forever—trusting in a kind of invisible arms race going on behind the scenes between the predators trying to reach us and the constantly updated defensive software companies have created to defend us. Through it all, we always return to the Web; indeed, it might be said that we respond by doubling down—both the Internet economy and the value of individual transactions have grown continuously now for two decades. Obviously, there is something in the technology itself that imbues us with a greater sense of trust than we experience in our dealings with the real world economy.

We can speculate on what that "something" is. One likely possibility might be called *calculation of risk:* we human beings—sometimes precisely, but often quite inaccurately—seem to naturally assign a coefficient of risk to everything we do. Walking into that beat-up shop in a sketchy neighborhood, we have a pretty good idea of the odds of getting ripped off. But what are the odds in cyberspace? We have only a rough idea of the total pool of our fellow potential victims—hundreds of millions?—and very little idea of how many crooks are out there—thousands? millions? So we tend to imagine ourselves comparatively secure from this kind of crime. And even when we are victims of it, we usually assume it is anomalous and after a brief interval go back to what we were doing before.

A second explanation might be called *technological immunity*. This is derived from Moore's Law and can be described as the belief, common to most of us, that any setback today in working with the Internet or other forms of technology will quickly be fixed through the rapid progress of technology itself. Got a virus? There'll soon be a patch, or a new upgrade in your security software, to defend against it. Ripped off? There's insurance, not to mention ratings systems that will tag the bad guys, and new software filters coming online from the retailer.

Underlying this is the unconscious assumption that somewhere out there, on your side, are law enforcement people and code writers who are more capable and more vigilant than the hackers, criminals, and terrorists who are trying to do you harm.

And so far, that assumption has paid off for most people most of the time.

Family Trust

The fourth, and final, new form of trust is one we have seen before—but which has returned in a radically different, almost unrecognizable, form in the digital age. Call it *Family Trust*, and it describes the unique relationships we have in the digital world with our personal online groups, tribes, and communities.

We will investigate this more in the next chapter, but for the moment it is important to recognize the uniquely *bipolar* nature of the Web world. On the one hand, the Internet is a deeply private medium, enabling us to link up with one another in our small, seemingly "personal" webs embedded in the vast global Web we scarcely notice. When we search for an item on eBay or Wikipedia, the act only seems intimate because we only have to look at the object of our interest, not the banks of encyclopedia volumes or the crowded, noisy flea market of the past.

At the same time—and we don't mean that just rhetorically, but literally *simultaneously*—the Web is also a truly public medium, in which almost every bit of data is potentially available for access by anyone. We get a brief glimpse of this each time we "Google" a topic and note that there are, say, 13 *million* listings related to it.

What's interesting about this is that even when we recognize this structural schizophrenia, we often tend to ignore it. Consider the number of employees caught every day looking at porn, gambling, or bidding on auctions using their office computer—and no amount of warnings about company surveillance seems to affect those numbers. Or the number of people arrested for describing, on blogs or in chat rooms, crimes they would never have admitted to in person.

But perhaps the most celebrated examples of this breakdown between the private and public spheres on the Web are the growing number of cases of young people who post photographs of illicit behavior on their MySpace and Facebook pages. The practice of using these photographs to damage the reputations— even forcing the resignations—of public figures such as Hollywood celebrities and beauty queens began almost from the moment these sites became popular in 2004. The media also quickly discovered that criminals and their victims often had pages on these sites and so began to mine them for photographs and other information. So did the growing number of Hollywood gossip sites.

One might imagine that this would have made the millions of other young people using Facebook and MySpace—as well as Friendster, Bebo, BlackPlanet, Classmates.com, and Orkut, to name just a few of the many online social networks around the world—a little more wary of what they posted on their pages. But just the opposite seemed to occur: these Web 2.0 communities were flooded with endless photos of young people in sexually compromising positions, taking drugs or committing various misdemeanors, even felonies. Even when stories began to appear about companies perusing these sites to vet job seekers, universities and colleges doing the same thing to help weed out applicants, and even high schools visiting their students' pages to look for illegal behavior, millions of young users *still* didn't purge their pages of incriminating material. They still don't.

Now, when human beings appear to do something inexplicable, when they seem to behave in a manner that is contrary to what should be their own best interests, the usual reasons are either that they are ignorant of the real risk, or that they see some other interest that eclipses the first.

In this case, we think it is both: young people know there is *some* risk to these photos catching up with them, but underestimate its magnitude (these searches are, in fact, becoming a standard tool of schools and businesses). Even then, they are willing to accept that risk because the present rewards for this behavior—social ranking, respect from friends, opportunity to meet new people, assertion of individuality and rebellion—are perceived as far greater than any future cost. These individuals trust that technology will protect their privacy, trust that their pages will be hard to find by anyone outside their immediate circle, and most of all trust that their actions will be accepted—even esteemed—by designated "friends" and other members of their immediate cyber-family, who will never rat them out.

Only the last is likely to be true.

Public and Private Communities

Earlier in this book we presented the case that the most valuable currency in the Web-based global economy will be Trust.

But the crucial lesson of this chapter is that Trust in the new economy is far from monolithic. In fact, it not only varies by geography and culture (as it always has), but also takes on unexpected new forms in the digital age.

To the business executive, the political leader, the marketer, the journalist, or the community activist this fragmentation of Trust itself offers both perils and opportunities.

On the one hand, Trust is the universal key to gain access to the inner circle of your targeted group. But the path to earning that Trust may not be clear—and you may waste time and money pursuing a form of acceptance that has little value to the people you are targeting.

This multiplicity of forms of Trust also means that there is no single approach that will work with *all* customers. Even worse: though the evidence is not yet in, there is even the potential nightmare scenario in which these fragmented, insular, clannish submarkets not only demand one of these different forms of Trust for entry, but might combine bits and pieces of one or more into an infinite number of permutations of Trust.

In either case, it seems inevitable that to meet this challenge, companies will have to fragment many of their own operations—marketing, marcom, sales, manufacturing, service, and support—in response, creating ad hoc corporate SWAT teams, like miniature corporate divisions, designed to target a key audience and then systematically penetrate its cultural defenses. In other words, *Companies (and other institutions) will have to atomize their own operations in order to succeed in a fragmented marketplace.*

This may seem like bad news—and for many companies that cannot adapt to this new order of things, it will be. But to aggressive and smart companies, it represents an extraordinary opportunity—and not just because it is a game-changer that will bring down many established and complacent enterprises and open the door to exciting new ones.

No, the real opportunity lies in the potential renaissance of *customer loyalty,* something that's been sorely lacking in our fast-moving, media-driven, and frenetic modern marketplace. The rise of the new fragmented global economy is not going to spell the end of impulse buying, fads, and one-hit wonders—on the contrary, with three billion consumers online these are likely to only increase. And, after all, none of us will be buried in our groups 24/7—we'll still surf the Web, watch television, and go to the mall. There will be vast fortunes to be made from what remains of the old economy.

It will be a land of entrepreneurs, promoters, and impresarios, more exciting than ever—but it will be a tough place to build an enduring enterprise. Consumers, in their billions, will flitter about, taking up one new fad even as they drop another.

But if you can manage to get *inside* the communities and "families" of the new economy, the landscape will be very different indeed. Suddenly, you become not only the first choice for the product or service you offer, but if it is properly tended, you can maintain that position almost indefinitely. You will also find that acceptance for business thrusts and directions is also easier to obtain. Even your failures will be given the benefit of the doubt. In essence, you will enjoy all of the advantages of being the official in-house supplier. Needless to say, that's a great place to be.

Of course, there are downsides to that as well—the biggest

being the anchor of *legacy*. Intense customer loyalty can be a heavy drag on innovation, as you turn away from riskier choices to focus on giving your base what it wants. And this in turn creates an odd picture of some companies, operating safely inside "private" market communities and seemingly moving in a comfortable slow-motion, while just outside the walls of that community other companies are blasting past, caught up in the continuous frenzy of the public marketplace.

It seems to us that crossing that divide between those two marketplaces will become more and more difficult over time—the "private" community company risking being run over if it steps outside those walls, the "public" marketplace company getting whiplash coming to a screeching halt entering into a community. It may one day be the case that a young company, almost from its founding, will have to choose one trajectory over another . . . and stick with it for the life of the enterprise.

Back Doors

How then do you get inside these communities in order to sell your products and services? And perhaps more important, how do you get inside hundreds of thousands of them, all of them with different entry requirements, *at the same time*?

We've already provided some answers—such as the use of bemes, the enlistment of members already inside these communities, the creation of customized products and services, and actual membership itself. With this chapter, we can add two more:

Structural Strategy: You need to build your enterprise or institution, from the get-go, specifically to fit with these niche communities in the new economy, as opposed to competing in the public marketplace. Once again, no size fits all—it will be almost impossible to build a company that competes both for niche communities *and* the global marketplace. But to focus on these niches will mean fragmenting your operations to become more fluid and adaptive, and emphasizing customization, service, and support even over innovation. In other words, to sell to a mass of niche bubbles, you will have to become the same thing.

Small to Big/Big to Small: Implicit in our discussion of the bipolarization of the new economy between small groups of individuals and the global community is the possibility that there is a *second* way into fragmented markets. Just as individuals use MySpace and Facebook to reach out to the larger world, often unconsciously, it should be possible to reverse the process, diving down from global networks and larger communities to obtain access to smaller groups and communities that reside there. Already, there are a host of companies out there, such as Facebook application provider Slide, that are developing tools and analytics to help companies find their way inside communities to the right customers and then quickly characterize them. Needless to say, even at its best, this technique will likely only get you to the addresses and the front doors of the thousands of groups you'll need to reach to build a business. After that, you will still have to reorganize your operations and implement the techniques we've already described (trust, customization, and so forth) to earn your way inside these groups.

You cannot look at all of these fundamental changes in the gestalt of the emerging global Internet-based economy and not appreciate that these changes will extend beyond the world of commerce into other areas of human existence. A new commercial order always creates a new social order.

What that new social order will look like, and how it will affect what it means to do business, to buy and sell and market goods, to be a producer and a consumer, and ultimately, to live and work in this new order, will be the subject of our concluding two chapters.

CHAPTER 11

THE QUESTION OF ORDER

Strategy for a Fragmented World

> What we imagine is order is merely the prevailing form of chaos.
>
> —KERRY THORNLEY

For a generation now, both business academics and futurists have been predicting that two fundamental forces—essentially epiphenomena arising from the digital and communications revolutions—will utterly transform the nature of business and work:

De-massification—The process by which companies and other organizations shift from fixed capital assets (buildings, factories, and so on) to increasingly virtualized infrastructures (intranets, home offices, virtual work teams), simultaneously resulting in a radical shift from centralization and central control to decentralization and the transfer of decision-making to the fringes. For consumers, this means a shift from mass-produced, homogeneous products and services to mass-customized experiences. It also means that these same consumers will be increasingly enlisted into the creation (and design and service) of these products and services.

The Death of the Middle—The hollowing of hierarchal organizations through the implementation of digital and communications technologies, which increasingly obviates the need for most traditional levels of middle management. The result is a "flattening" of the organization and an increase in management spans of control. For consumers, this often means using the Internet and digital intermediaries (cell phone, e-mail, instant messaging) to short-circuit traditional distribution and retail channels and purchasing directly from the manufacturer or a single intermediary.

These notions have been around so long that they have become not only familiar but cliché. Not surprisingly, when these predictions have not produced effects as sweeping as originally declared, there has also been something of a backlash. Thus, demassification neither gave us a world in which each of us designs everything from our homes to our cars to our television shows, nor did it allow all of us to leave the office forever and go work at Starbucks or in the extra bedroom at home. By the same token, the Middle endures: most of us still work for several layers of supervisors and managers, and we still shop at the neighborhood supermarket and at the local mall. Like personal helicopters, the "paperless" office, and personal robots—and all of those other giddy *Jetsons* predictions of a generation ago—these two trends seem mostly observed these days with irony.

But it is important now to note that there is another "law" of technology (that happens to be named after one of us), first enunciated more than a decade ago:

MALONE'S LAW: All technological revolutions arrive later than we expect, but sooner than we are prepared for.

In fact, much of the de-massification and the hollowing of the world's leading economies has already occurred—and right before our eyes. But because these transformations tend to start slowly and accelerate quickly, as well as because of the human tendency to assimilate incremental change without really noticing it, much of the transformation has barely registered in our consciousness.

But it is most certainly there. So, though we may not remember exactly when it happened that we stopped going to work every day, and began to spend a couple days each week at home with our laptops, it certainly happened at some point to most of us. And though most company executives in 1995 expressed serious doubt that they would ever let their employees work anywhere but at the office, most of those same managers were around a decade later to write the e-mails *ordering* those same employees to work at home in order to cut overhead.

And those memos went out just about the time those same managers decided that the best use of company talent and time was to create teams of designers, code writers, and others that either remain in situ at offices around the world, linked together via video and the Web, or operate in one location . . . and then at the end of the workday hand the project off to a mirror team eight time zones away—allowing work to continue around the clock.

By the same token, though it was little remarked at the time, beginning in the mid-1990s and often disguised by lay-offs or corporate reorganizations, middle management slowly began to disappear from corporate organization charts. It's hard for anyone under forty years old to remember, but historically a company lay-off almost exclusively meant the firing of rank-and-file workers. Management, at even the lowest supervisory position, was considered a secure position. That stopped being the case with the rise of corporate networks and Management Information Systems in the late 1980s; after that, the stripping away of middle management to reduce costs and even increase productivity became standard procedure. The trend only accelerated with the rise of the Web and wireless.

As a result, after all of the economic ups and downs and other vagaries of the last decade, we now find ourselves working in organizations with as little as one-third the management they began with—and we already accept this new reality as the status quo.

In other words, the revolution in corporate culture that we were promised, and that has so far largely disappointed us, has in fact already begun to arrive under the cover of apparent normalcy. And thus, we are currently living out the first half of Malone's Law—and feeling as if all of those Big Changes coming our way have turned out to be an overhyped dud.

But adoption curves, especially those driven by technological change, are usually exponential . . . and so, what starts out slowly (the disappointment phase) will suddenly ramp up fast until it seems to race out of our control (the overwhelmed phase). Hence the second part of Malone's Law: just when we think we have these changes under control, they suddenly accelerate beyond our ability to deal with them. After that, it may take a generation or more to catch up—and usually only when the pace of the revolution begins to slow.

Overwhelmed

You've probably already noticed that these two trends are absolutely congruent with the emerging global economy that we have been describing. The bipolar world of global interconnection counterbalanced by small clannish groups is the Death of the Middle writ large; while the shift from geographically based associations to online communities is the very definition of de-massification.

In other words, the emerging global, Internet-based economy we are describing in this book is essentially what happens when these two trends go asymptotic. And our new models for marketing, selling, and even working in this new world are ultimately a recipe for business survival once we enter the "overwhelmed phase."

The important questions to ask right now are:

What constitutes the "Middle"—and if you are in it, which way do you go: up or down?
How far will the de-massification process go—and what traditional business will remain?

These are not easy questions to answer, especially this early in the process. Once the turn is made and things take off quickly, the trajectory of this transformation will be much easier to measure and to predict from. Of course, by then it may be too late.

For now, we can only make some intelligent guesses, based upon what we've seen already (the rise of Web 2.0, the second and third billion consumers, Moore's Law, Metcalfe's Law that the value of a network increases exponentially with the number of users, the new smartphones like the Android-powered G1 and the iPhone, and the latest advances in long-distance wireless broadband such as WiMax and fourth-generation wireless G4) and on our experience with how people adopt radical new technologies.

Let's begin by developing a taxonomy of how businesses relate to the world around them. From this perspective, there are essentially five types of enterprises:

INTRINSICALLY LOCAL

These are businesses that are typically small, rarely serve more than the immediate neighborhood, and are often single-proprietor. You frequent them because the services they provide can only really be provided locally. Think barbershops, beauty salons, convenience stores, gas stations, restaurants, grocery stores, automobile repair shops. For the most part, these enterprises will not be affected at all by the new global economy. No matter how much the world is networked, you will still drive down the street to get a quart of milk.

HABITUALLY LOCAL

By comparison, these enterprises, though often assumed to be intrinsically local, are in fact highly vulnerable to an increasingly networked world—especially after the right technological revolution or a quantum leap in communications or delivery systems. Classic examples of this are the local printer, the video rental store, and the local record store—all of them were assumed to be enduring local operations—until they were rendered all but extinct by, respectively, desktop publishing, Netflix, and MP3 technology. The local hardware store, green grocer, and department store were all overwhelmed by improved distribution and inventory systems implemented by national chains.

The awful truth is that, with only a handful of exceptions, *every* local business and institution is under competitive risk from the newly emerging business order. You will still go to the local hospital, but your diagnosis, your lab analysis, and your X-ray reading may well be shipped electronically to doctors and technicians half a world away. Given some recent experimental tests, even *surgery* may one day be done remotely.

By the same token, it wouldn't take much in the way of physical delivery systems (as Amazon has already begun to do with dry goods) to obviate the need to go to the supermarket for anything but fresh produce (and even that is now being challenged by FreshDirect in some cities). By the same token, with a few improvements in modeling technology it might be possible to never again visit a car dealership or appliance store; or with better imaging techniques to never again visit a mall to buy jewelry, clothing, or sporting goods.

The history of the electronics revolution has been the half-century movement from analog processes to digital ones—the latter immediately enjoying the unmatched improvements of Moore's Law. A quarter-century ago, it was generally believed that perhaps 10 percent of the economy could cross over to the digital world. Today in a world of billions of embedded processors in everything from engines to pacemakers, that percentage may prove to be 80 to 90 percent.

In other words, anything that can go digital, ultimately will. And when something goes digital, it inevitably goes global. And the more things go digital, and the more they are rewarded with explosive growth, enhanced scale, and blindingly fast innovation, the more entrepreneurs will search through every little corner of an industry to find anything that can be digitized and turned into a new business.

There is no stopping this process. All that you can do is look very hard at your own business, strip away any preconceptions or habits you have about it, and determine what parts of it can go virtual (that is, digital). In other words, don't wait for the competition to show up from China, Mozambique, and down the street, but get there first and decide what kind of business you want to be. If you want to stay local, jettison that part of your business that wants to go global or it will remain vulnerable to competitors.

FRACTIONALLY LOCAL/GLOBAL

There are a number of companies—indeed, some of the most famous in the world—that are hybrids of global and local companies. Classic examples include the huge franchisers, such as McDonald's, KFC, and The Gap, and consumer electronics manufacturers such as Nokia and Apple.

These food and beverage giants would seem to serve as a counterargument to the claim that the economy is becoming increasingly bipolar. After all they are *both* global and local, somehow straddling those two worlds and successfully functioning in both realities.

But upon closer inspection, especially of the recent history of those companies, it becomes apparent that they too are not immune to the bifurcation of the new economy.

Consider McDonald's. This Southern California company, under Ray Kroc, became the most famous fast food company on the planet through a combination of a clean, standardized, and visually attractive store design, a limited menu of easily prepared items, a systematization of cooking and serving processes, and most of all economies of scale in distribution that resulted in consistent, quality products at a very low price.

It worked brilliantly, and within twenty years McDonald's stores not only had popped up all over America, but went on to conquer the world selling, famously, billions and billions of hamburgers. McDonald's also served as the template for numerous other franchised fast food shops—including KFC, Wendy's, and others—that themselves have become billion-dollar enterprises.

But though we often visualize these companies as monolithic, standardized, and homogeneous, one has only to visit a McDonald's in, say, Hong Kong or a KFC in Nairobi to appreciate that a lot has changed in the last twenty years. For example, a Big Mac is almost always available, but often the rest of the menu is dominated by local fare and favorites. And though you can still identify the Golden Arches, Ronald McDonald may be absent because of taboos about representative art. Meanwhile, billions of people may know KFC, but most these days don't know it stands for "Kentucky Fried Chicken"—or that the avuncular face, now stylized and half-hidden by the logo, belongs to founder Harland Sanders.

In other words, these global/local giants have hardly been immune to the increasingly bipolar nature of global business, their regional organizations shriveling in importance as they pull apart to become global operations whose task is increasingly that of providing standards and tools to local operations—not to make them more alike, but to empower them to become sufficiently localized without losing their core company culture.

Because it requires a tenuous combination of global control with local autonomy, this kind of business model is very difficult to maintain—and will become more so as even long-established markets become more demanding of local customization. This is especially true with food products, but other businesses are just as likely to see similar pressures, though often disguised—thus, the Sony Vaio laptop computer and Apple iPhone designs may be universal, but the languages they operate in, the programs they run, and the content they store are becoming more localized by the year—just look at the increasingly narrow (and in many cases, geographically and culturally specific) applications being designed for the latter. At some point, these local cultural differences may drive localized changes in the hardware as well—as regional differences in electrical power, plugs, keyboards, and formats already do.

With its unmatched global reach, McDonald's is likely to be a bellwether for many of these changes. And there we are already seeing some important clues: for example, not only has Mickey D's had to deal with wide variations in diets and popular foods among different cultures, but the company has also found itself unwillingly dragged into regional and global politics—at times serving as a synecdoche (and thus a target) for anti-Americanism.

Meanwhile, even McDonald's longtime safe and predictable domestic market has begun to revolt against its once-popular cookie-cutter approach. Most readers will have experienced in the last couple years the many changes the company has made—rotating menu items, upgraded interiors, health-oriented meals—or read about the company's efforts to convert some of its stores into sit-down restaurants or (to compete with Starbucks) add coffee bars, and so on. Clearly the direction McDonald's (and by extension, its competitors) is heading is toward a model that consists of a global headquarters operation that manages strategy, quality, global (but not local) distribution, branding, and image, and sets operating standards, presiding over thousands of local restaurants and franchisees enjoying considerable autonomy within those guidelines.

This all may sound reasonable, but it raises some troubling questions that may only be answered with time and experience:

How much autonomy should these local operations be given . . . and, as they listen more to their "family" of customers than to corporate headquarters, how easy will it be to rein them in?

How far will local operations be able to differ from the global "standard" and still be recognizable as part of the organization—in other words, when does a Mickey D's stop being a Mickey D's?

If local operations become too autonomous, what rewards and punishments does the parent company have left to control them—and what's to keep them from breaking off and becoming competitors?

What about the different operating speeds, levels of innovation, and commitment to customer retention between the parent company operating in the high-speed, chaotic global market and the local operation dealing with a loyal, change-averse customer base? Companies tend to worry about maverick local operations, but the real threat to the company's internal cohesion may in fact come from reactionary local operations with happy, loyal clients who don't want to implement all of the changes demanded by headquarters. How will global/local companies regularly cross the gap between fast-moving headquarters functions and slower-moving local operations?

HABITUALLY GLOBAL

The standard twenty-first-century view of business is that "going global" is a sign of success. The company that grows from humble beginnings as a local or regional business, then successfully takes its operations nationally, is inevitably judged as having crossed a major milestone in its history when it makes the leap to selling its products or services internationally.

But this attitude is merely a legacy of a different time, when the obstacles to going global were immense, and typically required an enterprise to first grow a large and financially powerful domestic base, then make massive capital expenditures to install the necessary manufacturing, sales, marketing, financial, and legal infrastructure to open subsidiaries in other countries.

But that is no longer true. The Internet provides much of that infrastructure, including various low-cost financial and legal applications (such as PayPal), to make this process of going global much simpler. Governments have done their own part by restraining themselves from over-taxing Internet commerce and embarking on campaigns to improve trade by simplifying paperwork.

The result is that it is now quite possible to skip the local, regional, and national steps in a company's evolution and go right to the international marketplace—and to do so for a matter of pennies.

Take the example of a poor farmer in Botswana. Once each week he may head down to the local stream, cut down some reeds and stick them in different-colored muds for a few days. Then, once the reeds are sufficiently stained dark brown, orange, or red, he'll spend his evenings weaving them into mats and rugs of different geometric designs.

Once he has a dozen of these rugs completed, he can set them out against a tree, photograph them with a smartphone he rented for a few hours from the nearby town, and then list them for sale *to an international audience* on eBay. Because there are hundreds of other mat makers in the area just like this man, there is almost no local demand for his products. And outside airport shops and a few tourist boutiques, there is little demand for his products in the country, either. Or for that matter, that part of sub-Saharan Africa. But there are customers for this beautiful native craft in Asia, America, and Europe—and now our poor Botswanan farmer can sell his wares to them directly with costs of less than a dollar per transaction.

Our farmer-weaver not only runs a global business—without ever having traversed the upward path through all the intermediate markets—but his business may be more naturally, *intrinsically* global than many of the great international enterprises that we assume fit into this category. We have just seen how businesses that have traditionally been considered local may in fact have components of their operations that, because they can be digitized and managed remotely, are in fact destined to become global—and that traditionally local enterprises may wake up to discover that they face ferocious new competitors not down the street but from the other side of the world.

By the same token, being a global company no longer confers immunity from competition by other all but global competitors. If we reverse our perspective, it becomes apparent that just as there is an imperative for the digital parts of a business to migrate to the global Web, so too is it true that the analog components have a natural tendency to revert to local control.

Becoming a global company confers some powerful advantages, especially when standardization allows for unbeatable economies of scale. But once those standardized products and services are assimilated by the various nations and cultures, expectations move on to something different or better.

If those changed expectations are universally the same—for example, the entire world wants another *Terminator* movie—then a business can be said to be Intrinsically Global (see p. 234). But far more likely is that the pressure will be toward greater customization to produce products and services more congruent with local interests, tastes, and needs. That's why you can buy fish and chips at the Oxford McDonald's and fish makes up half the menu at the Great Wall KFC in Beijing.

This suggests that there is a kind of maturation arc for habitually global companies that extends beyond the local/region/global pathway curve we already know about. It is that once a company goes global and remains there for a certain amount of time—probably one human generation now, perhaps less in the future as the economy speeds up—it will then be forced to trend backward toward increasingly customized, local operations, while perhaps still retaining a residual global organization, perhaps a holding company or a component distributor, to tie these local subsidiaries together.

Indeed, it is quite possible that the fate of some of these companies will actually be to shatter, atomizing into hundreds of independent local companies—their only link with the once world-spanning parent company that of a common name, trademark, or recipe (if even that).

INTRINSICALLY GLOBAL

In light of all of that, is there really such a thing as a company that is naturally, structurally, intrinsically global?

Here, once again, I think we have to break with twentieth-century preconceptions of what it means to be a global enterprise. The images of Nike, Pepsi, Royal Dutch Shell, Sony, Samsung, Toyota, and DHL, among others, has taught us to see global companies as being not only large, but *enduring*.

But once again, in the new, fragmented global economy, we have to abandon that preconception: just as the modern global company doesn't have to be large, neither does it have to be stable and enduring. In fact, just the opposite may be true: in a world increasingly characterized by small, family-like market bubbles floating in a vast and chaotic global marketplace, it may well be that what permanence and stability there is will be found at the local level, not the global.

Instead, the global marketplace is likely to be characterized in the future by the following:

▶ Large companies that evolve to global operations, but only stay there for a while before they continue to mature into networks of more localized subsidiaries;
▶ Evanescent firms that capture a fad or two, or market a hot new invention and briefly ride it to riches before disappearing back into the maelstrom;
▶ Entertainment entities that use the latest technology to mass-customize media to a global audience. These

enterprises will also be short-lived (or their content will be);

▶ Small businesses producing highly specialized goods that, because of the Internet, mobile communications, and modern delivery systems, can be easily sold to a global audience.

To these groups we can add, in answer to the question that began this section, certain companies and industries that do, by their very nature, appear to be naturally global: oil companies (though that could be changed by micro-power sources), financial institutions, telecommunications, certain airlines, and parcel delivery. But compared to the world we see around us today, these traditional global players will be reduced in numbers and very much a minority in the global marketplace. And, please note that it would only take a few technological advances—such as an efficient, low-cost micropower source—to render even some of these survivors less-than-intrinsically global.

Meanwhile, consider those four groups of enterprises that are most likely to dominate the new global marketplace. Different as they are, they have a number of characteristics in common. For one thing, unlike today's great multinationals, these new global players are likely to be physically quite small, with bare-bones staffs that can quickly ramp up (through contract employees, manufacturers, and distributors) to meet sudden and explosive demand. In other words, they are highly "virtualized" enterprises compared to their local counterparts.

Nearly all, even our poor Botswanan farmer, are almost entirely dependent upon the fickleness and changing tastes of the global audience. Demand can explode or evaporate in a matter of days, and so they must be prepared to deal with both. And (the farmer aside) they are also highly dependent upon the financial system to quickly provide the capital they need to ramp up to meet a sudden jump in demand, or a loan to get them through the next slump.

Most of all, in the long run, the odds are stacked against the new global companies. Lightning is unlikely to strike twice for these wildcatters, so they must hit hard and fast, make their money while they can and then be prepared to move on. In other words, unlike for their famous predecessors, going global for this new generation of companies means *greater* volatility, less control, and a far greater likelihood of failure . . . and sudden, immense fortune. Indeed, there are likely to be some real winners in this game—men and women, many of them from the developing world, and with a natural understanding of the next two billion consumers—who manage to string together a half-dozen of these "wins" in a row—and become history's first *trillionaires*.

A New Order

So there it is, at the end of the various technological, economic, demographic, and anthropological forces we currently see at work around us: a new Global Business Order. It is both strange and very different from what even our brightest pundits were predicting just a few years ago.

This New Order features some of the most unlikely business bedfellows one can imagine: the corner barber and a once-global, but now splintered, corporation competing at the neighborhood level, while global banks, fast-moving entertainment companies, and poor Third World artisans work side-by-side on the world stage. What has been largely stable and large (global business) becomes unpredictable and shrunken; while that which was volatile and local (small business) may become both predictable and suddenly capable of reaching around the planet. Giant companies may pretend to be tiny, while little firms may puff themselves up to look like world beaters.

As we have seen over and over in this book, the world economy being delivered by the Internet Age is nothing like the one we were promised. There is no global Kumbaya in the offing. And though the Web and universal wireless broadband will indeed enable us to reach out to everyone in the world, it will also work in the opposite direction—and force us to hide among friends in our little secure bubbles to escape the noise, chaos, and predators of this three-billion-strong global conversation.

The Internet promised a single global marketplace—and we will get just that. But it won't be anything like we expected. Instead of an expansion of the comparatively calm, largely rational global marketplace we enjoy today, it is more likely to resemble one vast flea market or Arab souk. Meanwhile, what we thought could be made obsolete by the World Wide Web—small, local businesses—are not only unlikely to succumb to some kind of supercharged cyber-Wal-Mart effect, but, transformed by technology and using Trust as their private currency, may actually thrive in this new landscape.

Everywhere we look in this new business world we will see this bipolarity at work, pulling enterprises in one direction or the other—small, trust-driven, customized, and careful, or global, fast-moving, and high-risk/high-reward. Almost everything in between will be hollowed out or stripped away. By the same token, enterprises themselves will find that the two sides of their organizations—the digital and the analog, the technological and the human, the universal and the personal—will also begin moving in opposite directions, threatening to pull them apart, forcing them to make crucial decisions on what strategy they want to pursue. For many companies these will not be easy decisions, but they must be made, because as the world economy begins to fragment, there will be little opportunity for the "either/or" or the "both."

Ultimately, and inevitably, this transformation will spill out beyond the world of business and begin to affect other institutions: nonprofits and NGOs, governments, communities, even families. If there is one truth about business revolutions it is that eventually they become social revolutions as well. As the reward structures change, as the nature of work changes, as the distribution of wealth changes, so too must society and culture change as well.

In a world characterized by a vast, frenzied global marketplace—an even more souped-up version of the pop/gossip world we live in today—intermixed with millions of small, closely knit groups defined by trust and common interests, who can doubt that we will see a comparable bipolarism reflected as well in our cultural institutions, our mores, and our values? In many ways, it will seem as if this new Global Order is just one great contradiction: sovereignty will be threatened *and* strengthened. Privacy will be battered *and* upheld. Trust will mean everything *and* nothing. Our little groups will be our world *except* when the whole world is.

Just as much as past economic transformations—though then as now we refused to see it coming—the New Global Order will transform how we work, play, and relate to one another, and how we define ourselves in the universe. And that can't help but change what we value, what we determine gives our lives sustenance and meaning.

And that will be the subject of our final chapter.

CHAPTER 12

THE HUNGER TO BELONG

Returning to Our Ancient Roots

Man—a being in search of meaning.
—PLATO

By now, the reader will probably have realized that the relentless push of technology—with the economy and society in its train—may also be painting each of us into a corner.

Or, more accurately, *two* corners: one being the small, safe (and hopefully well-stocked) fortress of microniches, the other the vast, sometimes dangerous world of a multimedia interconnected global market. And while there will be residual institutions left behind, for the most part there will be very little left in between these two antipodes.

If this is really the scenario of the future—and we believe it is—the two most important questions this book should provoke are *How do we possibly live in these two worlds simultaneously? And assuming that we can do so, how do we make such a life satisfactory and rewarding?*

It goes without saying that, for each of us, finding the answers to these questions is vitally important. But what makes the challenge even greater is that, given the pace of technological change, combined with the speed at which those next two billion consumers are entering the global marketplace, even if we do know the answers, we may still not be able to implement them in time. Speed, like everything else in this new world, is of the essence.

Pulled in Half

The first question—*How do we possibly live in these two worlds simultaneously?*—is easier to answer, though that answer may not be particularly satisfactory or comforting.

For a crude analogy to the world we are heading for, imagine you are sitting in a quiet parlor with your quilting club, a group of people you've known many years, and with whom you have so many things in common that you can almost finish one another's sentences. It is comforting, warm, and safe. But for some reason or another—career? shopping? curiosity? boredom?—you decide to get up from your comfy chair, walk to the front door and step out into . . .Times Square on New Year's Eve. Or the world's largest flea market. Or a million-person political protest.

Suddenly, you are in a sea of humanity. It's exciting, risky, sexy, enthralling, exhausting. You are surrounded by hawkers, barkers, gamblers, street musicians, pickpockets, and gangs. The best and worst of humanity, combined with every experience and sensation imaginable.

But take a step back through that doorway and it's back to the quilting club, the cup of tea, and the cat purring under your chair.

Unless there's a person out there who lives in a soundproof apartment in the French Quarter during Mardi Gras, Times Square on New Year's, or Rio during Carnival, there is nobody in the world who has experienced anything quite like this. And yet, in less than a decade, this is likely to be the daily experience of *most* of us.

If this seems like something out of a movie, perhaps that isn't surprising—film, by extrapolating and exaggerating daily life, is often a rehearsal for (or a warning about) the future. And, in fact, most of us already have had a glimpse of this new world barreling toward us: sitting in a quiet den, wearing a bathrobe, and drinking coffee . . . and finding ourselves emotionally and psychologically pulled into some event in the larger world—watching helplessly as a terrorist attack takes place, being deep in a bidding war with someone on the other side of the world in the last seconds of an auction, laughing at a viral video being watched by thousands of other people at the same moment, participating in a team of pseudonymous players in the middle of an online firefight.

This "other" world is compelling, captivating, and sometimes terrifying—a wonderful place to visit, but not somewhere most people would want to live. But home base, though comforting, is also likely to be stultifying for most of us if we are forced to stay there for any prolonged period of time.

So, perhaps the best answer to the question of how we will live in such radically different worlds simultaneously is that *we won't*. Instead, we will live in them serially, hopping back and forth between the two many times each day. And that means that in this new bipolar digital world most people—at work, at play, and even at school—will spend their lives making perpetual adjustments and negotiations, finding that "sweet spot" of the moment, the most satisfactory combination of time spent in their bubbles and out in the world. And, because few people will want to exclusively inhabit just one of these two worlds, the future is likely to exhibit considerable cultural pressure to allow individuals to easily migrate from one to the other—just as, today, many workers, based upon the professional and personal demands of a given week, modify the ratio of time they work at home and at the office.

Similarly, over an extended period of time, it is likely that most people will gravitate toward some consistent ratio of personal/public participation that will be a function of their careers, acculturation, and personalities.

Perhaps a more interesting question is, how, given the extremely different characteristics of these two worlds—fast/slow, anonymous/personal, expansive/intimate, risky/secure—will we make the transition back and forth between the two numerous times each day? Sometimes it will have to induce a kind of psychological whiplash, the equivalent of stepping from the sidewalk into a moving car, or jumping off a speeding train.

The answer is simple: we'll deal with these sudden transitions because *we'll want to*, because the emotional and economic rewards of being able to quickly move back and forth between the exhilarating global marketplace and the company of friends in a secure microniche will far exceed any wear and tear from the frequent journeys between them. No doubt it will be stressful on occasion—what in life isn't?—but hardly unprecedented. And human beings are remarkably resilient. Just a few generations ago, our grandparents and great-grandparents—the generational cohort born in the 1880s to 1890s—managed in their lifetimes to experience more change than any generation in human history. They were born in a world of oil lamps, horses, and locomotives yet lived to see computers, television, lasers, and men walking on the moon . . . and yet they seemed largely unfazed by the experience. What we face in the years ahead pales by comparison.

We'll muddle through, as we always have. And there's a good chance we'll even like this new world better than the one we live in now.

Integration

Once we inhabit this new world and become accustomed to it, it likely won't seem bipolar at all. Once we've found our own best ratio between public and private, the global marketplace and our select microniches, and make it second nature to hop back and forth between them, they will seem less distinct than interlocking. There will no longer be here and there, but private, calm, and long-standing atriums within the larger mass marketplace.

Interestingly, it was a similar notion of a stable core in the midst of a cloud of frenetic and constantly evolving activity that coauthor Michael S. Malone arrived at while trying to puzzle out the paradox of creating highly adaptive companies that are nevertheless stable and enduring. The result was the book *The Future Arrived Yesterday*—and his description of what he called the "Protean" corporations of the future.

The Future was essentially a follow-up to Malone's (and venture capitalist Bill Davidow's) 1992 bestseller *The Virtual Corporation*—with the benefit of nearly fifteen years of reconsideration. *The Virtual Corporation* and similar books of that era—*Mass Customization, When Giants Learn to Dance, Re-Engineering the Corporation*—have been hugely influential in showing corporate executives that the arrival of computers and telecommunications had made it possible for them to reorganize their companies to be more adaptive, edgeless, and empowering of individual employees. In response, companies had flattened their organizations, installed massive information networks, moved decision making down the org chart, sent many of their employees home to work, enlisted customers into product design and service, and entered into much deeper and more integrated strategic partnerships with suppliers and distributors.

The result, particularly for the early adopter companies, was explosive growth and capture of dominant market share. And, indeed, the rise of "virtualized" corporations in the 1990s was one of a number of critical factors in the competitive economic success of the United States in the 1990s. Moreover, with the advent of the World Wide Web in general usage—the ultimate "virtual" tool—these theories seemed particularly prescient.

But there was something not quite *right* about virtual corporations, a structural weakness that only became more evident as the years went on. And, after more than a decade of reporting on these companies, when Malone sat down at last to write *The Future Arrived Yesterday*, he had a very good idea of just what that weakness was:

Virtual corporations *had no heart.*

The reader can find a more complete explanation elsewhere, but for our purposes the simple summary of the problem is this: by virtualizing their organizations, executives made their companies more adaptive and dynamic, but they also hollowed out their centers, losing much of their corporate cultures in the process. When half of the employees are working at home, or at Starbucks, at any given moment; when many of those employees have never visited corporate headquarters—or even met their team members in person; when it is hard to distinguish among employees, contractors, part-timers, and visiting employees from other companies; and when the company itself becomes nebulous and edgeless—then an essential part of what it means to be a "company" fades away.

The company begins to lose its history, its culture, and ultimately its identity. Employees no longer feel part of a larger movement, of a crusade. And when tough times arrive, there is really nothing left in the company—the employee loyalty and self-identification, the sense of duty to the past, even the feeling of momentum—that makes the company worth sacrificing for, much less saving. For all of their adaptability and success, virtual corporations can be empty places where no amount of working at home and employee empowerment can compensate for their unique loneliness.

The question is, How do you retain the unequaled adaptability of virtual corporations—a hugely competitive advantage in the fast-moving modern economy—with the need to create an enduring, permanent "heart" within their walls? In other words, how do you create a shapeshifter (that is, "protean") company that is, at the same time, enduring and unchanging?

It would appear to be a paradox. And yet, just such contradictions exist in the natural world: no matter how much it changes its appearance, a chameleon remains a chameleon. Our bodies replace every cell over the course of seven years, yet we retain our "selves." So, perhaps it might be possible after all to create a corporate organization that is simultaneously transitory and permanent.

The solution comes in the form of a small, permanent "Core"—in this case, employees with a deep, lifelong commitment to the company—surrounded by a "Cloud" of workers ranging from longtime employees to contractors who might work for the company online for just a matter of minutes writing a line or two of code.

To work in the Core of such a Protean Corporation means lifetime employment, a deep sense of loyalty and participation, and considerable power. But the cost is the surrender of the ability to move about freely, the opportunity to control your destiny, and the chance to take risks. By comparison, out in the Cloud lies excitement, entrepreneurial opportunity, and freedom—but at the cost of security, predictability, and continuity.

Sound familiar? Of course: it is the microniche/global market model, the bubbles-in-a-roiling ocean model of the new global economy we've been describing throughout this book. Perhaps that's not surprising given the authors—but Malone came to his model of the Protean Corporation, and he and Tom Hayes to the theme of this book, from opposite directions.

Now, combine this with the advent of "cloud computing" (mass computation taking place on hundreds or thousands of individual small computers); with a million small microloans being made by a bank with only a few thousand employees; with social networks racing toward a billion members but run by only a few dozen employees—and you have a possible glimpse of the future. And what we may be seeing is the birth of new metaphors to define the era: tiny clusters (bubbles, cores) of enduring purpose immersed in vast, fast-moving clouds of events (protean organizations, the global Internet economy).

We may also be glimpsing for the first time the defining image of our time: *foam in a swirling sea.*

The Hunger to Belong

The modern economy has created many miracles: extended our life spans, opened up all of the knowledge of the world to the average person, enabled us to easily speak to anyone on the planet—and in perhaps the greatest miracle of all, lifted one quarter of the world's chronically poor out of poverty in just the last decade.

These are achievements with almost no parallel in human history. But it has come at a cost—and perhaps the biggest is that it has increasingly stripped us of our traditional sense of *belonging*. Five thousand years of human civilization built an astonishingly long list of institutions—family, neighborhood, states, nations, clubs and organizations, churches—that acted as intermediaries between us as individuals and mankind as a whole.

But with the Death of the Middle, almost every one of those

institutions is now either irrelevant or under assault. Meanwhile, thanks to access, scope, and speed never before available, each of us finds ourselves increasingly drawn toward the global market-place (for example, eBay and Amazon), polling place (the blogo-sphere, surveys), and theatrical stage (YouTube, Hulu). The image of the solitary Web surfer sitting in a darkened room, linked to events unfolding around the world, but unconscious of what is going on just outside, is no longer just a cliché—no doubt every reader of this book knows a person (probably a teenager) who is just like that. As we've already noted, one of the strang-est phenomena of the modern world is the individual who feels more at home in a virtual neighborhood, and with other mem-bers of a virtual work team, than in his or her real neighborhood and office.

There is one school of technology utopians who have sug-gested that this virtual world—and the global marketplace it has created—is basically all that we really need. Moore's Law and Metcalfe's Law, as well as advances in wireless communications, displays, and online financial instruments, they say, will soon make it possible for us to access, virtually and online, such a broad and rich array of experiences—travel, sex, art, commerce, medicine, sports, entertainment, education . . . indeed, more than was available to monarchs five hundred years ago—that there will be little need for the close, real-life connections of the past.

The best refutation of that argument is a considerable body of sociological, psychological, and anthropological evidence pro-vided earlier in this book—all of which says that, simply put, "people need people." We need them physically proximate—and when that isn't possible, we need them close enough virtually to bond with them over common interests. And that bonding needs to take place in a place of mutual trust, away from the back-ground noise of billions of shouting voices; it needs to occur between a small number of people whose limit seems organically fixed; and it needs to take place over an attenuated period so that the nuances of this trusting relationship can be worked out and strengthened.

But if that evidence isn't conclusive, then we need to merely look anecdotally at our own lives and those of people we know. Other than perhaps a few young people just out of school, it's hard to imagine any mature adult who could derive sufficient psychic sustenance from a life largely lived on the Web. On the contrary, almost anyone we know or have read about (obsessive gamers, for example) who even approaches that lifestyle is inevitably emotionally stunted, has emotional problems, or is spiraling down with self-destruction. A life lived adrift on the great digital ocean is literally no life at all. There is no place to *belong*.

So whatever source of emotional sustenance this new world might offer will have to come from the other side of the coin: the "bubbles" we have chosen to inhabit.

This shouldn't come as a surprise: from the beginning we have suggested that microniches—along with the surviving social structures of the physical world, such as family and neighborhood—are precisely the places where we will do most of our emotional interaction with others.

All well and good, but some very important questions remain:

How many of these small groups are we likely to join, and how will we manage this engagement?

What will these groups demand of us in terms of admission requirements, participation, and time?

How will these groups most likely be structured?

How will they enforce membership, including exiling dysfunctional or inactive members?

What is the life expectancy of one of these groups?

Finally, and perhaps most important, will these groups

provide enough emotional support, in conjunction with the remaining traditional social groups, to offer us the hope of satisfying and fulfilling lives?

These are not easy questions, and this early in the process any answers can only be speculative at best. But there are already some clues out there if we look for them. And as we close this book and enter this compelling new world, let's follow a few of those clues to see where they lead us.

Let's begin at the top. Obviously, the number of virtual groups that each of us is likely to join is the product of a calculus determined by the number of hours each group will require from us per week divided into the total number of hours we have available for this type of activity—minus the time we will be spending on nonvirtual group activities.

Unfortunately, this calculation isn't as easy as it may appear at first glance. For one thing, we don't really know the value of each of these variables yet. For example, the amount of time that virtual groups demand of their members is probably less than required by real-life groups—especially when you factor in such things as travel time to and from meetings. But, conversely, online groups may require more time for the socialization that normally takes place drinking coffee and waiting for everyone to arrive, in the parking lot after the meeting, and so on.

Even the amount of time available for our "bubbles" is still unclear. For one thing, unlike most real-life activities, virtual participation can go on well into the late hours of the night as we surf the Web in a bathrobe from the comfort of the laptop in the den. Then there's the matter of multitasking: it's pretty difficult to be part of a stamp club while you're at the bowling alley with your office team—but as any modern teenager easily proves, it's very easy to do a half-dozen activities at a time in the many windows on a computer screen. Finally, there is the tumbling traditional wall between work and play, office and home: in the new digital world we may be just as likely to be part of microniche groups at the office as we are at home—something that isn't nearly as true with traditional common-interest groups.

That said, it is also unlikely that these real-life groups will ever fully disappear. Some will survive—like the bowling team, our children's sports leagues, the local chapter of the VFW, and book groups—either because there is no acceptable virtual substitute (yet), or simply because we need (though how much is also not yet clear) to be around other flesh-and-blood people.

But even if we can't come up with a definitive number, it nevertheless seems likely that we will belong to *more* virtual groups than we ever have real-life ones—if only because they will be easier to maintain (though not necessarily easier to join), the selection will be vastly greater than now (where we are typically limited to opportunities in our community), and the process of search and discovery will be much easier.

How many real-life groups do most of us actively participate in now? We suspect the average is about ten—say, Patrick O'Brian fiction fans, alumni of Arizona State, psoriasis sufferers of Northern Colorado, '68 Volkswagen Bug owners, Fenton "hobnail" glass owners, Troop 466 BSA parents group, Renaissance Weekend/Hilton Head discussion group #14, morel mushroom cultivators, Friends of Children's Town AIDS orphanage in Zambia. That suggests the number of "bubbles" in our future lives will number some multiple of that: twenty? thirty? Only time will tell.

How hard will it be to join these future groups? Certainly a lot harder than it is right now—or at least as it was until recently. We are already seeing a hardening of membership requirements on many social sites—indeed, it was the perceived open access of MySpace to predators and other dangerous types that is credited with driving many members to Facebook, where they could protect themselves with "friends lists" and other protocols. LinkedIn has taken these safeguards still further by combining a more difficult admission requirement with invitation-only linkages.

In the emerging new world, where trust—and the security it creates—will be among the most valuable of commodities, membership requirements are inevitably going to become a whole lot stricter. Most will no doubt require sponsorship by an existing member and some sort of proof of competence, or at least interest, in the topic or project. There will also undoubtedly be much more vetting of applicants, and probably probation periods before full membership.

And that's only for groups that are still growing. Once they approach Dunbar's number or its equivalent, they will—strategically or unconsciously—begin to tighten up the admission process, as the addition of a new member will essentially mean the exile of an existing one. Established "bubbles" are probably going to look a lot like mature book clubs, investment groups, or private poker nights—in other words, someone is going to have to die before you can join.

As we've seen with real-life groups, one way that online groups will remain vital and regenerate with fresh blood will be to make ongoing membership requirements more demanding—and thus weeding out the insufficiently committed or the consistently contrary. We are already seeing this kind of behavior beginning to appear in the large community sites, news aggregators, and bulletin boards, where "trolls" are quickly identified, singled out, and ultimately banned by moderators. Some sites, such as Newsvine, will "excommunicate"—via a Code of Honor and a rating system of fellow users—trolls from most of the social groups that use the site. Digg does the same, but will allow the unpopular poster to be reinstated by a countervote.

It's unlikely, given the high barrier to entry that most of these bubbles will have, that there will be too many trolls popping up—but certainly the tools are already in place for dealing with them. And one can imagine, as with the small, introverted communities of old (such as the Puritan colonies, aboriginal villages, and monasteries), those who violate the rules or rarely participate in community life will find themselves shunned and eventually exiled. For the groups, this punishment will allow for the entry of other, more committed members. For the exiles . . . well, the good news is that the cost isn't starvation or being marooned, but merely the effort required to join another group or to create one of their own.

On the matter of how these groups will be structured, the easy answer is that, because the membership rolls aren't likely to get larger than human beings are able to deal with in one-to-one relationships, any kind of infrastructure will be necessarily quite simple. Real-life groups typically have a leader/president, vice president, recording secretary to disseminate information, a treasurer, and various committee leaders. Much of that, as most of us have already discovered, is unnecessary with virtual groups. There may be a team leader/moderator, with a designated backup, but because of universal access they are unlikely to be absent very often. These groups will be unlikely to have assets or dues, so unless the group is dedicated to charitable fund-raising or travel, a treasurer is also probably superfluous. As is a secretary, since all conversations and transactions will be automatically recorded. There may still be committees, with leaders, but they are also likely to be more provisional and ad hoc.

In all, the bubbles of the future—even those related to work, which will be more likely to have project goals, timetables, and reporting requirements—are going to be less structured and "flatter" than most groups we know today. In most groups, just about everyone will know everyone else, and just about everyone will be able to confidently speak for the group, knowing its position on most things.

Interestingly, they will also likely have close affinities to other, related groups—especially the ones that spun off from the "mother" group when it grew too large in the past. The process of spinning off will not be easy, and no doubt many groups will try to stay together and grow a lot larger. But human nature almost always wins in the end, and if groups don't happily divide at the proper time, they will likely do so unhappily later on. Either way, the fault line for this schism will probably be quite apparent as the members begin to congregate in smaller groups to keep their numbers down. Far better, then, that the split is amicable and done, as in the Amazonian tribes, at a predetermined time—that way some groups will have the option of remaining right-sized forever, while others can operate within a constellation of groups with a common pedigree (and none of the guilt and pressure of waiting lists).

The flattening of structure inside millions of microniche bubbles is likely to have a secondary effect on other organizations as well. The Core of Malone's Protean Corporation is also described as essentially structureless, with minimal leadership and nearly all members operating more or less as equals. So too will be the briefly lived bubbles that form as intrapreneurial (that is, enterprises created within existing organizations) endeavors, founded by impresario-like "Competence Aggregators," in the Cloud of the Protean Corporation. By the same token, all large organizations, as they increasingly resemble gigantic clusters of hundreds, even thousands, of bubbles, are likely to find traditional management superstructures unwieldy and irrelevant.

The global economy, as it becomes more "effervescent," like a carbonated sea of bubbles, will require fewer of the hierarchical structures needed to manage it now. Thus we will see even more hollowing of the middle in the society of the future.

By this point, it should be pretty apparent that "no size fits all" also describes the nature of these microniche bubbles. Just as in the real world, groups form around any number of different common interests and motives, from hobbies to political activism to social networking to sports teams to self-help, the range of bubble types—because of the sheer scope and range of the Web—is likely to be much greater. It's pretty hard to form a real-life group around an arcane topic—the Confederate marines, historic COBOL programs, fear of glass, Theosophy, the plays of Aristophanes, Stan Musial collectibles—because the locatable population of like-minded people is simply too small and diffuse to assemble. But on the Web there are very few topics that don't have thousands of adherents. And now there are even the tools, such as Ning, to bring them together.

Just as the nature of these bubbles is almost infinitely mutable, so too will be their duration. It's easy to imagine a group of product designers, until then strangers, who are drawn together by a Craigslist ad to spend just a few hours tackling some component packaging . . . then breaking apart to never work together again. Or a group of like-minded citizens forming a group to advocate for a local zoning matter being voted on by the city council a week hence, mobilizing support . . . then after the vote, splitting up—to perhaps come together again in a different configuration for another civic matter.

By the same token, there is also no reason why a group might not cluster around a topic such as the preservation of Nan (Bushman) culture or heirloom tomatoes or supporting the local museum . . . and stay together for decades. The group might even last longer than a human lifetime, as old members retire or die and new young members join.

Moreover, because nothing on the Internet ever really dies, it is also quite possible that groups could die, or at least go into suspended animation, leaving all of their records intact—to be picked up again by the original members, or a whole group of new members, years or decades later.

The Enduring Heart

Finally, the most important question of all, the one that ultimately determines whether this new world will be both sustainable and endurable:

Will these groups provide enough emotional support that, in conjunction with the remaining traditional social groups, they will offer us the hope of satisfying and fulfilling lives?

If not, then this new world will never have the time to mature and strengthen before its internal contradictions and failures force the next transformation. In other words, yet another period of growing frustration, followed by the demand to start over again. Nobody wants that.

So it all comes down to this. The global, Internet-driven marketplace is going to provide us with all of the excitement, stimulation, danger, opportunity, entertainment, and products and services we can ever want. It's going to be everything we have now—and much more.

Fifty years ago, that might have seemed enough. But we have learned, often to our dismay, that having almost everything—especially access to information and to one another—doesn't necessarily bring happiness. We still retain the fundamental, atavistic need to connect deeply with one another, to belong to something greater than ourselves, to be part of a group and be part of its story. Only the players on the other side of the new economy, the microniche bubbles, have the potential to provide for those needs.

Can they?

We don't know. Not yet, and probably not for a generation.

There are some obvious inherent weaknesses to these microniche bubbles. For one thing, there are certain disadvantages to being part of a virtual group compared to real-life ones. For example, part of the appeal of being in a group is the hardship of getting there—that's why there are initiation ceremonies and special awards for commitment. That pretty much evaporates when all you have to do is sign in online. One can also imagine that some groups, by becoming increasingly insular and introverted, could also become paranoid, fearful of the outside world, and increasingly cultlike. But perhaps the biggest risk would be that, by retreating from the outside world, they would become insular, oppressive, and resistant to chance and the random, unexpected events that make life richer.

Some of these fears, we think, are a bit overblown. The potential for these groups to become too insular is probably lower than in real life simply because, no matter how deeply a person might be engaged in one virtual group or another, his or her physical body still has to live in the physical world. As for level of commitment: that will actually be far easier to measure in the online world—cumulative time in the group, actual contribution to discussions and projects, group leadership—than in most real-life work teams, clubs, or organizations. And finally, no matter how insular a single group might be, its members will not only belong to numerous other groups but will also have to regularly wade out into the global marketplace—experiences that will keep just about anyone from being too cloistered away.

But it isn't enough to challenge the potential problems with microniche bubbles. There are also some decisive factors in their favor—enough, in fact, to offer considerable hope for the success of this new model.

For one thing, because groups will be mostly self-selecting, self-defining, and self-regulating, their potential to "fit" their members—especially if there are enough of these groups to offer an enormous selection—is extremely high. Certainly, it will be better than in most real-life groups, where the membership is usually as much defined by geographic proximity as by any real commonality.

Also, because they draw upon a pool of a millions of potential members (even billions, as English becomes the lingua franca of the world), the chances of finding—or building—just the right handful of groups for one's life is far greater than anything possible now. Furthermore, the transparency of the Internet, combined with the increasingly difficult admission requirements, will likely make most groups far more secure than real-life ones are now. And because of the interlinked nature of the Web, it will be a whole lot easier to find these groups.

But the single biggest advantage to this world of millions of bubbles arising in a swirling global market is that the experience is *mass customizable*.

Mass customization, if you remember, was one of the key advantages to the virtual corporation. The idea was that, using the power of computers and communications—and especially by enlisting the customers themselves in design and/or execution—it would be possible to deliver goods and services that were uniquely fitted to those customers.

It certainly worked, ending the century-long reign of mass production. Today we live in a largely mass-customized economy, in which we assist in the design of everything from our shoes to our cars to our clothes and homes; we design our entertainment experiences via TiVo and our iPod, and we use our computers and other tools to participate in everything from medical self-diagnosis to our public image (via Facebook, Twitter, and the like).

The power of the newly emerging fragmented global economy is that it extends mass customization to our *lives*. We no longer have to adapt ourselves to the existing structures of society, but through a perpetual process of group selection and participation, combined with an ongoing balancing act between the private world of bubbles and the public world of the global Internet marketplace, we make society adapt to *us*.

What is the psychological value of that kind of control and freedom? Each of us has to answer that question for ourselves, but it is hard not to believe that this new social and economic order will be an immense net positive for humanity. Our original question didn't ask for guarantees of happiness, but only the "hope" of satisfying and fulfilling lives.

We believe it does just that—and far better than what we have now.

Masters of Our Fate

We began this book with the notion of a fragmentation of the Internet-based global market. As the centerpiece of the book we proposed the image of a bipolar global economy, divided between a frenetic global market and millions of small, stable niche communities. And in the process we explored the underlying anthropological, cultural, and technological reasons why this is occurring now.

We also looked at the challenge for business of marketing to this new economic order, especially the need for new techniques and tools to penetrate the sturdy walls of the small microniche "bubbles."

We then moved beyond the structure of this new, fragmented marketplace and how, ultimately, it will also transform society itself. We then showed that new forms of living, of work and play, ultimately reflect backward upon the way people live and how they address the world, how they change their homes, their institutions, and their lifestyles.

And now we close with perhaps the most compelling image of all: that of this new Internet-based economy, with its unprecedented combination of the global and the personal, the vast and open countered by the small and private, presenting each of us with the opportunity for another dimension in human freedom: the full-scale customization of our own lives and experiences, based upon ambitions, desires, and needs.

In other words, to become the directors, the authors, the *entrepreneurs*, of our own lives . . . and enjoy both the freedom, and the responsibility, that brings. This great transformation has been brought about not only by technological change, but by our increasingly frustrated desire to connect, to *belong* to something that matters. And the irony is that at the end of this search we may find that "one size" that uniquely fits each of us—and enjoy the chance to at last connect—to belong—to ourselves.

ACKNOWLEDGMENTS

Writing a book about radical social and business change is an ambitious task, and we are grateful to the many people who in one way or another helped shape our thinking or supported our effort.

First, we are grateful to the many business leaders and colleagues who helped us think through our theses and arguments or otherwise kept us sharp as we wrote the book. For their insights and guidance we thank Marc Andreessen and Gina Bianchini, Rich Karlgaard, Arianna Huffington, Evan Williams and Biz Stone, Santosh Jayaram, Raymond Nasr, Reid Hoffman, Cyril Balas, Thierry Lamouline, Sehat Sutardja, and Weili Dai.

We thank the remarkable team at Penguin/Portfolio, led by Adrian Zackheim, and are particularly grateful to our editor, David Moldawer, for his clearheaded counsel and practical advice throughout.

Our agent, Jim Levine at LevineGreenberg, once again showed why he is the best in the business. His early thinking helped us shape the final product and we look forward to many more books together.

Finally, no effort of this scope would be possible without the forbearance and encouragement of family, and both authors want to acknowledge the steadfast support we received from our loved ones. Tom wishes to thank his mother-in-law, Marol Martin, for her invaluable support during the writing of the book, as well as the sustaining affections of his children, Samuel, Elizabeth, and Emerson, and his beautiful wife (and world-class writer in her own right), Estelle Hayes. Mike wishes to thank his wife, Carol, and his sons Patrick (Tad) and Tim (Skip) for their enduring patience in living their days and nights with a writer pacing about the house. He also thanks the people of Silicon Valley for their ideas and inspiration.

INDEX